COMFORTABLE WITH
UNCERTAINTY

BOOKS AND AUDIO BY PEMA CHÖDRÖN

BOOKS

Always Maintain a Joyful Mind
Awakening Loving-Kindness
Comfortable with Uncertainty
The Compassion Box
No Time to Lose
The Places That Scare You
The Pocket Pema Chödrön
Practicing Peace in Times of War
Start Where You Are
When Things Fall Apart
The Wisdom of No Escape

AUDIO

Comfortable with Uncertainty
Don't Bite the Hook
Perfect Just As You Are
Practicing Peace in Times of War: Four Talks
Start Where You Are
This Moment Is the Perfect Teacher
When Things Fall Apart
The Wisdom of No Escape

COMFORTABLE
with
UNCERTAINTY

*108 Teachings on Cultivating
Fearlessness and Compassion*

Pema Chödrön

Compiled and edited by
Emily Hilburn Sell

SHAMBHALA
Boston & London
2003

SHAMBHALA PUBLICATIONS, INC.
Horticultural Hall
300 Massachusetts Avenue
Boston, Massachusetts 02115
www.shambhala.com

15 14 13 12 11

Printed in the United States of America

⊗ This edition is printed on acid-free paper that meets the
American National Standards Institute z39.48 Standard.
♻ This book was printed on 30% postconsumer recycled paper.
For more information please visit us at www.shambhala.com.
Distributed in the United States by Random House, Inc.,
and in Canada by Random House of Canada Ltd

THE LIBRARY OF CONGRESS CATALOGS THE HARDCOVER
EDITION AS FOLLOWS:
Chödrön, Pema.
Comfortable with uncertainty: 108 teachings/Pema Chödrön; compiled
and edited by Emily Hilburn Sell.
p. cm.
ISBN 978-1-57062-972-3 (hardcover)
ISBN 978-1-59030-078-7 (paperback)
1. Spiritual life—Buddhism. 2. Meditation—Buddhism. 3. Buddhism—
Doctrines. I. Sell, Emily Hilburn. II. Title.
BQ7805 .C485 2002
294.3'444—dc21   2002003894

*May all sentient beings enjoy happiness
and the root of happiness.*

*May we be free from suffering
and the root of suffering.*

*May we not be separated from the great
happiness devoid of suffering.*

*May we dwell in the great equanimity free
from passion, aggression, and prejudice.*

CONTENTS

EDITOR'S PREFACE

THIS BOOK CONTAINS 108 practical teachings gathered from the works of Pema Chödrön. They are 108 pith instructions on leading our lives in the spirit of mahayana Buddhism. *Mahayana* means the "greater vehicle," the path that gradually leads us out of our cramped world of self-preoccupation into the greater world of fellowship with all human beings. The teachings selected here give a glimpse of the mahayana vision, a taste of the meditation practices it offers, and hints on carrying the vision and meditation into everyday life.

Pema draws from a long lineage of teachers and teachings. Her style is unique, but nothing she teaches is uniquely hers. Her teaching is particularly influenced by her own root guru, Chögyam Trungpa Rinpoche. Trungpa Rinpoche was one of the first Tibetans to present Buddhism to Westerners in English, combining the wisdom of the Kagyü and Nyingma lineages of Tibetan Buddhism with that of the kingdom of Shambhala. Shambhala is a legendary enlightened society rooted in the view of basic goodness, the practice of meditation, and the activity of cultivating bodhichitta, the awakened heart of loving-kindness and compassion. The story goes that the first king of Shambhala received teachings from the Buddha, practiced them, and passed them on to his subjects. Rinpoche called this secular meditative tradition "the sacred path of the warrior," emphasizing the inherently awake quality ("basic goodness") of ourselves and our surroundings. Meditation practice is how we discover basic goodness and learn to cultivate bodhichitta. With this view, practice, and activity, even the most mundane situation becomes a vehicle for awakening.

Because they are rooted in universal principles and everyday practicalities, these teachings have survived a long time—at least twenty-five hundred years. They are not dogmatic. Students are continually encouraged to test them and to experience their truth (dharma) for themselves. For this reason, these teachings are highly adaptable. They are able to speak in any language and to any culture. Pema Chödrön continues the Shambhala Buddhist tradition of Trungpa Rinpoche by bringing the ancient discipline of Buddhism and the warrior tradition of Shambhala into the modern-day culture and psyche.

In essence, these teachings tell us that by cultivating mindfulness and awareness, we can realize our inherent wealth and share it with others. This inner treasure is called bodhichitta. It is like a jewel buried deep within us—ours to unearth as soon as the conditions are ripe. Bodhichitta is often presented in two aspects: absolute and relative. Absolute bodhichitta is our natural state, experienced as the basic goodness that links us to every other living being on the planet. It has many names: openness, ultimate truth, our true nature, soft spot, tender heart, or simply what *is*. It combines the qualities of compassion, unconditional openness, and keen intelligence. It is free from concepts, opinions, and dualistic notions of "self" and "other."

Although absolute bodhichitta is our natural state, we are intimidated by its unconditional openness. Our heart feels so vulnerable and tender that we fabricate walls to protect it. It takes determined inner work even to see the walls, and a gentle approach to dismantling them. We don't have to tear them down all at once or "go at them with a sledgehammer," as Pema puts it. Learning to rest in openhearted basic goodness is a lifelong process. These teachings offer gentle and precise techniques to help us along the way.

Relative bodhichitta is the courage and compassion to investigate our tender heart, to stay with it as much as we can, and gradually to expand it. The key point of cultivating relative bodhichitta is to keep opening our hearts to suffering without shutting down. Slowly we learn to uncover the limitless qualities of love, compassion, joy, and equanimity, and to extend them with others. To train in making our hearts this big takes bravery and kindness.

There are several practices that help us open our hearts to ourselves and to others. The most basic of these is sitting meditation, which allows us to become familiar with the groundlessness and spaciousness of our nature. Another key practice is mind training (*lojong* in Tibetan), our inheritance from the eleventh-century Buddhist master Atisha Dipankara. Mind training includes two elements: sending-and-taking practice (*tonglen* in Tibetan), in which we take in pain and send out pleasure, and slogan practice, in which we use pithy slogans to reverse our habitual attitude of self-absorption. These methods instruct us in using what might seem like our greatest obstacles—anger, resentment, fear, jealousy—as fuel for awakening.

In this book Pema teaches sitting meditation, tonglen, working with slogans, and the aspiration practices of the four limitless qualities as gateways to the awakened heart of bodhichitta. With a daily practice of sitting meditation, we become familiar with our natural openheartedness. We begin to stabilize and strengthen ourselves in it. Off the meditation cushion, in everyday life, we then begin to experiment with keeping our hearts open even in the face of unpleasant circumstances. With tonglen and slogan practice we start to taste the flavor of what we fear and move toward what we habitually avoid. To further stretch our limits and open our hearts, we practice expanding the four limitless qualities—loving-kindness (*maitri* in Sanskrit), compassion, joy, and equanimity—by aspiring to extend them to others.

In addition, we can engage in particular activities (*paramitas* in Sanskrit) that take us beyond our strange human tendency to protect ourselves from the joy of our awakened heart. Pema calls these activities "the six ways of compassionate living": generosity, patience, discipline, exertion, meditation, and prajna, or wisdom. The basis for all these practices is the cultivation of maitri, an unconditional loving-kindness with ourselves that says, "Start where you are."

In Buddhist terms, this path is known as bodhisattva activity. Simply put, a bodhisattva is one who aspires to act from an awakened heart. In terms of the Shambhala teachings, it is the path of warriorship. To join these two streams, Pema likes to use the term warrior-bodhisattva, which implies a fresh and forward-moving energy that is willing to enter into suffering for others' benefit. Such action relates to overcoming the self-deception, self-protection, and other habitual reactions that we use to keep ourselves secure—in a prison of concepts. By gently and precisely cutting through these barriers of ego, we develop a direct experience of bodhichitta.

What everyone on this path shares is the inspiration to rest in uncertainty—cheerfully. The root of suffering is resisting the certainty that no matter what the circumstances, uncertainty is all we truly have. Pema's teachings encourage us to experiment with becoming comfortable with uncertainty, then see what happens. What we call uncertainty is actually the open quality of any given moment. When we can be present for this openness—as it is always present for us—we discover that our capacity to love and care for others is limitless.

For readers who have already received meditation instruction, the teachings in this book can serve as daily, weekly, or monthly reminders of key points on the path. For those who have not yet begun meditating, the book is intended as news you can use—not as a substitute for personal meditation instruction. The list of resources at the end of the book will help interested readers find a meditation instructor.

Thanks to Tingdzin Ötro, Tessa Pybus, Julia Sagebien, John and David Sell, Pema's transcribers, and the staff of Shambhala Publications—especially Eden Steinberg—for encouragement and support in this project. We are all grateful to Pema for embodying the path of a warrior-bodhisattva and for transmitting it in such an appropriate and timely way.

These 108 teachings are excerpted from longer discussions in Pema's previous books. In arranging them, I visualized them as a crystal bead with 108 facets, to be contemplated as you wish. May they be of measureless benefit.

Emily Hilburn Sell

The Love That Will Not Die

Spiritual awakening is frequently described as a journey to the top of a mountain. We leave our attachments and our worldliness behind and slowly make our way to the top. At the peak we have transcended all pain. The only problem with this metaphor is that we leave all others behind. Their suffering continues, unrelieved by our personal escape.

On the journey of the warrior-bodhisattva, the path goes down, not up, as if the mountain pointed toward the earth instead of the sky. Instead of transcending the suffering of all creatures, we move toward turbulence and doubt however we can. We explore the reality and unpredictability of insecurity and pain, and we try not to push it away. If it takes years, if it takes lifetimes, we let it be as it is. At our own pace, without speed or aggression, we move down and down and down. With us move millions of others, our companions in awakening from fear. At the bottom we discover water, the healing water of bodhichitta. Bodhichitta is our heart—our wounded, softened heart. Right down there in the thick of things, we discover the love that will not die. This love is bodhichitta. It is gentle and warm; it is clear and sharp; it is open and spacious. The awakened heart of bodhichitta is the basic goodness of all beings.

The Healing Power of Bodhichitta

Bodhichitta is a Sanskrit word that means "noble or awakened heart." Just as butter is inherent in milk and oil is inherent in a sesame seed, the soft spot of bodhichitta is inherent in you and me. It is equated, in part, with our ability to love. No matter how committed we are to unkindness, selfishness, or greed, the genuine heart of bodhichitta cannot be lost. It is here in all that lives, never marred and completely whole.

It is said that in difficult times, it is only bodhichitta that heals. When inspiration has become hidden, when we feel ready to give up, this is the time when healing can be found in the tenderness of pain itself. Bodhichitta is also equated, in part, with compassion—our ability to feel the pain that we share with others. Without realizing it we continually shield ourselves from this pain because it scares us. Based on a deep fear of being hurt, we erect protective walls made out of strategies, opinions, prejudices, and emotions. Yet just as a jewel that has been buried in the earth for a million years is not discolored or harmed, in the same way this noble heart is not affected by all of the ways we try to protect ourselves from it. The jewel can be brought out into the light at any time, and it will glow as brilliantly as if nothing had ever happened.

This tenderness for life, bodhichitta, awakens when we no longer shield ourselves from the vulnerability of our condition, from the basic fragility of existence. It awakens through kinship with the suffering of others. We train in the bodhichitta practices in order to become so open that we can take the pain of the world in, let it touch our hearts, and turn it into compassion.

3

Comfortable with Uncertainty

Those who train wholeheartedly in awakening bodhichitta are called bodhisattvas or warriors—not warriors who kill but warriors of nonaggression who hear the cries of the world. Warrior-bodhisattvas enter challenging situations in order to alleviate suffering. They are willing to cut through personal reactivity and self-deception. They are dedicated to uncovering the basic, undistorted energy of bodhichitta.

A warrior accepts that we can never know what will happen to us next. We can try to control the uncontrollable by looking for security and predictability, always hoping to be comfortable and safe. But the truth is that we can never avoid uncertainty. This not-knowing is part of the adventure. It's also what makes us afraid.

Wherever we are, we can train as a warrior. Our tools are sitting meditation, tonglen, slogan practice, and cultivating the four limitless qualities of loving-kindness, compassion, joy, and equanimity. With the help of these practices, we will find the tenderness of bodhichitta in sorrow and in gratitude, behind the hardness of rage and in the shakiness of fear. In loneliness as well as in kindness, we can uncover the soft spot of basic goodness. But bodhichitta training offers no promise of happy endings. Rather, this "I" who wants to find security—who wants something to hold on to—will finally learn to grow up.

If we find ourselves in doubt that we're up to being a warrior-in-training, we can contemplate this question: "Do I prefer to grow up and relate to life directly, or do I choose to live and die in fear?"

4

The Wisdom of No Escape

The central question of a warrior's training is not how we avoid uncertainty and fear but how we relate to discomfort. How do we practice with difficulty, with our emotions, with the unpredictable encounters of an ordinary day? For those of us with a hunger to know the truth, painful emotions are like flags going up to say, "You're stuck!" We regard disappointment, embarrassment, irritation, jealousy, and fear as moments that show us where we're holding back, how we're shutting down. Such uncomfortable feelings are messages that tell us to perk up and lean into a situation when we'd rather cave in and back away.

When the flag goes up, we have an opportunity: we can stay with our painful emotion instead of spinning out. Staying is how we get the hang of gently catching ourselves when we're about to let resentment harden into blame, righteousness, or alienation. It's also how we keep from smoothing things over by talking ourselves into a sense of relief or inspiration. This is easier said than done.

Ordinarily we are swept away by habitual momentum. We don't interrupt our patterns even slightly. With practice, however, we learn to stay with a broken heart, with a nameless fear, with the desire for revenge. Sticking with uncertainty is how we learn to relax in the midst of chaos, how we learn to be cool when the ground beneath us suddenly disappears. We can bring ourselves back to the spiritual path countless times every day simply by exercising our willingness to rest in the uncertainty of the present moment—over and over again.

Loving-Kindness: The Essential Practice

For an aspiring bodhisattva, the essential practice is to cultivate maitri, or loving-kindness. The Shambhala teachings speak of "placing our fearful mind in the cradle of loving-kindness." Another image for maitri is that of a mother bird who protects and cares for her young until they are strong enough to fly away. People sometimes ask, "Who am I in this image—the mother or the chick?" The answer is we're both: both the loving mother and those ugly little chicks. It's easy to identify with the babies—blind, raw, and desperate for attention. We are a poignant mixture of something that isn't all that beautiful and yet is dearly loved. Whether this is our attitude toward ourselves or toward others, it is the key to learning how to love. We stay with ourselves and others when we're screaming for food and have no feathers and also when we are more grown up and more appealing by worldly standards.

In cultivating loving-kindness, we learn first to be

honest, loving, and compassionate toward ourselves. Rather than nurturing self-denigration, we begin to cultivate a clear-seeing kindness. Sometimes we feel good and strong. Sometimes we feel inadequate and weak. But like mother-love, maitri is unconditional; no matter how we feel, we can aspire that we be happy. We can learn to act and think in ways that sow seeds of our future well-being. Gradually, we become more aware about what causes happiness as well as what causes distress. Without loving-kindness for ourselves, it is difficult, if not impossible, to genuinely feel it for others.

Loving-Kindness and Meditation

When we start to meditate or to work with any kind of spiritual discipline, we often think that somehow we're going to improve, which is a subtle aggression against who we really are. It's a bit like saying, "If I jog, I'll be a much better person." "If I had a nicer house, I'd be a better person." "If I could meditate and calm down, I'd be a better person." Or the scenario may be that we find fault with others. We might say, "If it weren't for my husband, I'd have a perfect marriage." "If it weren't for the fact that my boss and I can't get on, my job would be just great." And, "If it weren't for my mind, my meditation would be excellent."

But loving-kindness—maitri—toward ourselves doesn't mean getting rid of anything. Maitri means that we can still be crazy, we can still be angry. We can still be timid or jealous or full of feelings of unworthiness. Meditation practice isn't about trying to throw ourselves away and become something better. It's about befriending who we are already. The ground of practice is you or me or whoever we are right now, just as we are. That's what we come to know with tremendous curiosity and interest.

Curiosity involves being gentle, precise, and open—actually being able to let go and open. Gentleness is a sense of goodheartedness toward ourselves. Precision is being able to see clearly, not being afraid to see what's really there. Openness is being able to let go and to open. When you come to have this kind of honesty, gentleness, and good-heartedness, combined with clarity about yourself, there's no obstacle to feeling loving-kindness for others as well.

7

Why Meditate?

As a species, we should never underestimate our low tolerance for discomfort. To be encouraged to stay with our vulnerability is news that we can use. Sitting meditation is our support for learning how to do this. Sitting meditation, also known as mindfulness-awareness practice, is the foundation of bodhichitta training. It is the home ground of the warrior-bodhisattva.

Sitting meditation gives us a way to move closer to our thoughts and emotions and to get in touch with our bodies. It is a method of cultivating unconditional friendliness toward ourselves and for parting the curtain of indifference that distances us from the suffering of others. It is our vehicle for learning to be a truly loving person.

Gradually, through meditation, we begin to notice that there are gaps in our internal dialogue. In the midst of continually talking to ourselves, we experience a pause, as if awakening from a dream. We recognize our capacity to relax with the clarity, the space, the open-ended awareness that already exists in our minds. We experience moments of being right here that feel simple, direct, and uncluttered.

This coming back to the immediacy of our experience is training in unconditional, or absolute, bodhichitta. By simply staying here, we relax more and more into the open dimension of our being. It feels like stepping out of a fantasy and discovering the simple truth.

8

The Six Points of Posture

Sitting meditation begins with good posture. Awareness of the six points of posture is a way to be really relaxed and settled in our body. Here are the instructions:

1. *Seat*: Whether you're sitting on a cushion on the floor or in a chair, the seat should be flat, not tilting to the right or left, or to the back or front.

2. *Legs*: The legs are crossed comfortably in front of you—or, if you're sitting in a chair, the feet are flat on the floor, with the knees a few inches apart.

3. *Torso*: The torso (from the head to the seat) is upright, with a strong back and an open front. If sitting in a chair, it's best not to lean back. If you start to slouch, simply sit upright again.

4. *Hands*: The hands are open, with palms down, resting on the thighs.

5. *Eyes*: The eyes are open, indicating the attitude of

remaining awake and relaxed with all that occurs. The eye gaze is slightly downward and directed about four to six feet in front of you.

6. *Mouth*: The mouth is very slightly open so that the jaw is relaxed and air can move easily through both the mouth and nose. The tip of the tongue can be placed on the roof of the mouth.

Each time you sit down to meditate, check your posture by running through these six points. Anytime you feel distracted, bring your attention back to your body and these six points of posture.

9

No Such Thing As a True Story

By weaving our opinions, prejudices, strategies, and emotions into a solid reality, we try to make a big deal out of ourselves, out of our pain, out of our problems. But things are not as solid, predictable, or seamless as they seem.

In sitting meditation, our practice is to watch our thoughts arise, label them "thinking," and return to the breath. If we were trying to find the beginning, middle, and end of each thought, we'd soon discover that there is no such thing. Trying to find the moment when one thought becomes another is like trying to find the moment when boiling water turns into steam. Yet we habitually string our thoughts together into a story that tricks us into believing that our identity, our happiness, our pain, and our problems are all solid and separate entities. In fact, like thoughts, all these constructs are constantly changing. Each situation, each thought, each word, each feeling, is just a passing memory.

Wisdom is a fluid process, not something concrete that can be added up or measured. The warrior-bodhisattva trains with the attitude that everything is a dream. Life is a dream; death is a dream; waking is a dream; sleeping is a dream. This dream is the direct immediacy of our experience. Trying to hold on to any of it by buying our story line only blocks our wisdom.

Sitting Meditation

Meditation practice is a formal way in which you can get used to lightening up. I encourage you to follow the instructions precisely, but within that form to be gentle. Let the whole thing be soft. Breathing out, touch your breath as it goes. Sense the breath going out into big space and dissolving. You're not trying to clutch or catch that breath, you're simply relaxing outward with it. There's no particular instruction about what to do during the in-breath—there's nothing to hold on to until the next out-breath.

Labeling our thoughts during meditation practice is a powerful support that reconnects us with the fresh, open, unbiased dimension of our mind. When we become aware that we are thinking, we say to ourselves, "thinking," with an unbiased attitude and with tremendous gentleness. Then we return our focus to the breath. We regard the thoughts as bubbles and the labeling like touching them with a feather. There's just this light touch—"thinking"—and they dissolve back into the space. Even if you still feel anxious and tense when the thoughts go, simply allow that feeling to be there, with space around it. Just let it be. When thoughts come up again, see them for what they are. It's no big deal. You can loosen up and lighten up.

Saying "thinking" is an interesting point in the meditation practice. It's the point at which we can consciously train in gentleness and in developing a nonjudgmental attitude. Loving-kindness is unconditional friendliness. So each time you say to yourself "thinking," you are cultivating unconditional friendliness toward whatever arises in your mind. Since this kind of unconditional compassion is difficult to come by, such a simple and direct method for awakening it is exceedingly precious.

Four Qualities of Maitri

Meditation takes us just as we are, with our confusion and our sanity. This complete acceptance of ourselves as we are is a simple, direct relationship with our being. We call this maitri. There are four qualities of maitri that are cultivated when we meditate:

1. *Steadfastness.* When we practice meditation we are strengthening our ability to be steadfast with ourselves, in body as well as mind.

2. *Clear seeing.* Clear seeing is another way of saying that we have less self-deception. Through the process of practicing the technique day in and day out, year after year, we begin to be very honest with ourselves.

3. *Experiencing our emotional distress.* We practice dropping whatever story we are telling ourselves and leaning into the emotions and the fear. We stay with the emotion, experience it, and leave it as it is, without proliferating. Thus we train in opening the

fearful heart to the restlessness of our own energy. We learn to abide with the experience of our emotional distress.

4. *Attention to the present moment.* We make the choice, moment by moment, to be fully here. Attending to our present-moment mind and body is a way of being tender toward self, toward other, and toward the world. This quality of attention is inherent in our ability to love.

These four factors not only apply to sitting meditation, but are essential to all the bodhichitta practices and for relating with difficult situations in our daily lives. By cultivating them we can start to train as a warrior, discovering for ourselves that it is bodhichitta, not confusion, that is basic.

The Root of Suffering

What keeps us unhappy and stuck in a limited view of reality is our tendency to seek pleasure and avoid pain, to seek security and avoid groundlessness, to seek comfort and avoid discomfort. This is how we keep ourselves enclosed in a cocoon. Out there are all the planets and all the galaxies and vast space, but we're stuck here in this cocoon. Moment after moment, we're deciding that we would rather stay in that cocoon than step out into that big space. Life in our cocoon is cozy and secure. We've gotten it all together. It's safe, it's predictable, it's convenient, and it's trustworthy. If we feel ill at ease, we just fill in those gaps.

Our mind is always seeking zones of safety. We're in this zone of safety and that's what we consider life, getting it all together, security. Death is losing that. We fear losing our illusion of security—that's what makes us anxious. We fear being confused and not knowing which way to turn. We want to know what's happening. The mind is always seeking zones of safety, and these zones of safety are continually falling apart. Then we scramble to get another zone of safety back together again. We spend all our energy and waste our lives trying to re-create these zones of safety, which are always falling apart. That's the essence of samsara—the cycle of suffering that comes from continuing to seek happiness in all the wrong places.

13

Weather and the Four Noble Truths

In the Buddha's first teaching—called the four noble truths—he talked about suffering. The first noble truth says that it's part of being human to feel discomfort. Nothing in its essence is one way or the other. All around us the wind, the fire, the earth, the water, are always taking on different qualities; they're like magicians. We also change like the weather. We ebb and flow like the tides, we wax and wane like the moon. We fail to see that like the weather, we are fluid, not solid. And so we suffer.

The second noble truth says that resistance is the fundamental operating mechanism of what we call ego, that resisting life causes suffering. Traditionally it's said that the cause of suffering is clinging to our narrow view, which is to say, we are addicted to ME. We resist that we change and flow like the weather, that we have the same energy as all living things. When we resist, we dig in our heels. We make ourselves really solid. Resisting is what's called ego.

The third noble truth says that suffering ceases when we let go of trying to maintain the huge ME at any cost. This is what we practice in meditation. When we let go of the thinking and the story line, we're left just sitting with the quality and the energy of whatever particular "weather" we've been trying to resist.

The essence of the fourth noble truth is that we can use everything we do to help us to realize that we're part of the energy that creates everything. If we learn to sit still like a mountain in a hurricane, unprotected from the truth and vividness and the immediacy of simply being part of life, then we are not this separate being who has to have things turn out our way. When we stop resisting and let the weather simply flow through us, we can live our lives completely. It's up to us.

14

The Facts of Life: Impermanence

According to the Buddha, the lives of all beings are marked by three characteristics: impermanence, egolessness, and suffering or dissatisfaction. Recognizing these qualities to be real and true in our own experience helps us to relax with things as they are. The first mark is impermanence. That nothing is static or fixed, that all is fleeting and changing, is the first mark of existence. We don't have to be mystics or physicists to know this. Yet at the level of personal experience, we resist this basic fact. It means that life isn't always going to go our way. It means there's loss as well as gain. And we don't like that.

We know that all is impermanent; we know that everything wears out. Although we can buy this truth intellectually, emotionally we have a deep-rooted aversion to it. We want permanence; we expect permanence. Our natural tendency is to seek security; we believe we can find it. We experience impermanence at the everyday level as frustration. We use our daily activity as a shield against the fundamental ambiguity of our situation, expending tremendous energy trying to ward off impermanence and death. We don't like it that our bodies change shape. We don't like it that we age. We are afraid of wrinkles and sagging skin. We use health products as if we actually believe that *our* skin, *our* hair, *our* eyes and teeth, might somehow miraculously escape the truth of impermanence.

The Buddhist teachings aspire to set us free from this limited way of relating to impermanence. They encourage us to relax gradually and wholeheartedly into the ordinary and obvious truth of change. Acknowledging this truth doesn't mean that we're looking on the dark side. What it means is that we begin to understand that we're not the only one who can't keep it all together. We no longer believe that there are people who have managed to avoid uncertainty.

15

Not Causing Harm

Learning not to cause harm to ourselves or others is a basic Buddhist teaching. Nonaggression has the power to heal. Not harming ourselves or others is the basis of enlightened society. This is how there could be a sane world. It starts with sane citizens, and that is us. The most fundamental aggression to ourselves, the most fundamental harm we can do to ourselves, is to remain ignorant by not having the courage and the respect to look at ourselves honestly and gently.

The ground of not causing harm is mindfulness, a sense of clear seeing with respect and compassion for what it is we see. This is what basic practice shows us. But mindfulness doesn't stop with formal meditation. It helps us relate with all the details of our lives. It helps us see and hear and smell without closing our eyes or our ears or our noses. It's a lifetime's journey to relate honestly to the immediacy of our experience and to respect ourselves enough not to judge it. As we become more wholehearted in this journey of gentle honesty, it comes as a shock to realize how much we've blinded ourselves to some of the ways in which we cause harm.

It's painful to face how we harm others, and it takes a while. It's a journey that happens because of our commitment to gentleness and honesty, our commitment to staying awake, to being mindful. Because of mindfulness, we see our desires and our aggression, our jealousy, and our ignorance. We don't act on them; we just see them. Without mindfulness, we don't see them and they proliferate.

16

The Dharma

The dharma—the Buddha's teaching—is about letting go of the story line and opening to *what is*: to the people in our life, to the situations we're in, to our thoughts, to our emotions. We have a certain life, and whatever life we're in is a vehicle for waking up.

Often we hear the teachings so subjectively that we think we're being told what is true and what is false. But the dharma never tells us what is true or what is false. It just encourages us to find out for ourselves. However, because we have to use words, we make statements. For example, we say, "The everyday practice is simply to develop complete acceptance of all situations, emotions, and people." That sounds like to do this is what's true and not to do this would be false. But that's not what it means. What it means is that we could find out for ourselves what is true and what is false.

Try to live that way and see what happens. You'll come up against all your doubts and fears and hopes, and you'll grapple with that. When you start to live that way—with that sense of "what does this really mean?"—you'll find it quite interesting. After a while, you forget that you're even asking the question. You just practice meditation or you just live your life, and you have insight—a fresh take on what is true. Insight comes suddenly, as though you've been wandering around in the dark and someone switches on all the lights and reveals a palace. It's been there all along. It feels as if we've discovered something that no one else ever knew, and yet it's completely straightforward and simple.

17

The Practice of Mindfulness and Refraining

Refraining is very much the method of becoming a dharmic person. It's the quality of not grabbing for entertainment the minute we feel a slight edge of boredom coming on. It's the practice of not immediately filling up space just because there's a gap.

An interesting practice that combines mindfulness and refraining is just to notice your physical movements when you feel uncomfortable. When we feel like we're losing ground, we make all kinds of little jumpy, jittery movements. You might notice that when you feel uncomfortable you do things like pull your ear, scratch something even though it doesn't itch, or straighten your collar. When you notice what you do, don't try to change it. Don't criticize yourself for whatever it is you're doing. Just notice what it is.

Refraining—not habitually acting out impulsively— has something to do with giving up the entertainment mentality. Through refraining, we see that there's something between the arising of the craving—or the aggression or the loneliness or whatever it might be—and whatever action we take as a result. There's something there in us that we don't want to experience, and we never do experience, because we're so quick to act. The practice of mindfulness and refraining is a way to get in touch with basic groundlessness—by noticing how we try to avoid it.

18

Relax As It Is

It's helpful to always remind yourself that meditation is about opening and relaxing with whatever arises, without picking and choosing. It's definitely not meant to repress anything, and it's not intended to encourage grasping, either. Allen Ginsberg used the expression "surprise mind." You sit down and—wham!—a rather nasty surprise arises. So be it. This part is not to be rejected but compassionately acknowledged as "thinking" and let go. Then—wow!—a very delicious surprise appears. Okay. This part is not to be clung to but compassionately acknowledged as "thinking" and let go. The surprises are endless. Milarepa, the twelfth-century Tibetan yogi who sang wonderful songs about the proper way to meditate, said that the mind has more projections than there are dust motes in a sunbeam and that even hundreds of spears couldn't put an end to that. As meditators we might as well stop struggling against our thoughts and realize that honesty and humor are far more inspiring and helpful than any kind of solemn religious striving for or against anything.

In any case, the point is not to try to get rid of thoughts, but rather to see their true nature. Thoughts will run us around in circles if we buy into them, but really they are like dream images. They are like an illusion—not really all that solid. They are, as we say, just thinking.

19

Working with Slogans

To reverse ego's logic, we practice the warrior slogans of Atisha, a Tibetan teacher who lived in the eleventh century. These slogans say things like, "Don't be jealous," and you think, "How did they know?" Or "Be grateful to everyone"; you wonder how to do that or why to bother. Some slogans, such as, "Always meditate on whatever provokes resentment," exhort you to go beyond common sense. These slogans are not always the sort of thing that you would want to hear, let alone find inspiring.

If we work with the slogans, they will become like our breath, our eyesight, our first thought. They will become like the smells we smell and the sounds we hear. We can let them permeate our whole being. That's the point. These slogans aren't theoretical or abstract. They are about who we are and what is happening to us. They are completely relevant to how we experience things, how we relate with whatever occurs in our lives. They are about how to relate with pain and fear and pleasure and joy, and how those things can transform us fully and completely. When we work with the slogans, ordinary life becomes the path of awakening.

20

Slogan: *"All activities should be done with one intention"*

Breathing in, breathing out, feeling resentful, feeling happy, being able to drop it, not being able to drop it, eating our food, brushing our teeth, walking, sitting—whatever we're doing could be done with one intention. That intention is that we want to wake up, we want to ripen our compassion, and we want to ripen our ability to let go, we want to realize our connection with all beings. Everything in our lives has the potential to wake us up or to put us to sleep. Allowing it to awaken us is up to us.

21

Turning Arrows into Flowers

On the night the Buddha was to attain enlightenment, he sat under a tree. While he was sitting there, the forces of Mara shot arrows at him to distract him from becoming enlightened, but with awareness he turned their weapons into flowers.

Traditional teachings on the forces of Mara describe the nature of obstacles and how human beings habitually become confused and lose confidence in their basic wisdom mind. The teachings on the four maras provide descriptions of some very familiar ways in which we try to avoid what is happening. Like the Buddha, it is possible for us to turn these arrows into flowers. Rather than trying to get rid of an obstacle or buying into a sense of being attacked, we can use it to see what we do when we're squeezed. Do we close down or open up? Do we feel resentful or do we soften? Do we become wiser or more stupid?

1. *Devaputra mara* involves seeking pleasure. Any obstacle we encounter has the power to pop the bubble of reality that we have come to regard as secure and certain. When we're threatened that way, we can't stand to feel the edginess, the anxiety, the heat of anger rising, the bitter taste of resentment. Therefore, we reach for whatever we think will blot it out. We try to grasp something pleasant. The way to turn this arrow into a flower is to open our hearts and look at how we try to escape. We can use pleasure-seeking as an opportunity to observe what we do in the face of pain.

2. *Skandha mara* has to do with how we try to re-create ourselves when things fall apart. We return to the solid ground of our self-concept as quickly as possible. Trungpa Rinpoche used to call this "nostalgia for samsara." When things fall apart, instead of struggling to regain our concept of who we are, we can use it as an opportunity to be open and inquisitive about what has just happened and what will happen next. That is how to turn this arrow into a flower.

3. *Klesha mara* is characterized by strong emotions. Instead of letting feelings be, we weave them into a story line, which gives rise to even bigger emotions. We all use emotions to regain our ground when things fall apart. We can turn this arrow into a flower

by using heavy emotion as a way to develop true compassion for ourselves and everyone else.

4. *Yama mara* is rooted in the fear of death. We are killing the moment by controlling our experience. We want to hold on to what we have. We want every experience to confirm us and congratulate us and make us feel completely together. We say the yama mara is fear of death, but it's actually fear of life. We can turn this arrow into a flower by using the desire to control as a reminder to experience each moment completely new and fresh. We can always return to basic wisdom mind.

22

Nothing Solid

Moving away from our experience, moving away from the present moment with all our habits and strategies, always adds up to restlessness, dissatisfaction, unhappiness. The comfort that we associate with concretizing and making things solid is so transitory, so short-lived.

Moving into our experience—whether it's the opening experience of love and compassion or the closing-down experience of resentment and separation—brings us an enormous sense of freedom: the freedom of nothing solid. Something about "nothing solid" begins to equal freedom. In the meantime, we discover that we would rather feel fully present to our lives than be off trying to make everything solid and secure by engaging our fantasies or our addictive patterns. We realize that connecting with our experience by meeting it feels better than resisting it by moving away. Being on the spot, even if it hurts, is preferable to avoiding. As we practice moving into the present moment this way, we become more familiar with groundlessness, a fresh state of being that is available to us on an ongoing basis. This moving away from comfort and security, this stepping out into what is unknown, uncharted, and shaky—that's called liberation.

23

The Facts of Life: Egolessness

The second mark of existence is egolessness, sometimes called *no-self*. These words can be misleading. They don't mean that we disappear—or that we erase our personality. Egolessness means that the fixed idea that we have about ourselves as solid and separate from each other is painfully limiting. That we take ourselves so seriously, that we are so absurdly important in our own minds, is a problem. Self-importance is like a prison for us, limiting us to the world of our likes and dislikes. We end up bored to death with ourselves and our world. We end up very dissatisfied.

We have two alternatives: either we take everything to be sure and real, or we don't. Either we accept our fixed versions of reality, or we begin to challenge them. In Buddha's opinion, to train in staying open and curious—to train in dissolving the barriers that we erect between ourselves and the world—is the best use of our human lives.

In the most ordinary terms, egolessness is a flexible

identity. It manifests as inquisitiveness, as adaptability, as humor, as playfulness. It is our capacity to relax with not knowing, not figuring everything out, with not being at all sure about who we are, or who anyone else is, either. Every moment is unique, unknown, completely fresh. For a warrior-in-training, egolessness is a cause of joy rather than a cause of fear.

24

Staying in the Middle

Openness doesn't come from resisting our fears but from getting to know them well. We can't cultivate fearlessness without compassionate inquiry into the workings of ego. So we ask ourselves, "What happens when I feel I can't handle what's going on? What are the stories I tell myself? What repels me and what attracts me? Where do I look for strength and in what do I place my trust?"

The first thing that takes place in meditation is that we start to see what's happening. Even though we still run away and we still indulge, we see what we're doing clearly. We acknowledge our aversions and our cravings. We become familiar with the strategies and beliefs we use to fortify our cocoon. With mindfulness as our method we start to get curious about what's going on. For quite a long time, we just see it clearly. To the degree that we're willing to see our indulging and our repressing clearly, they begin to wear themselves out. Wearing out is not exactly the same as going away.

Instead, a wider, more generous, more enlightened perspective arises.

How we stay in the middle between indulging and repressing is by acknowledging whatever arises without judgment, letting the thoughts simply dissolve, and then going back to the openness of this very moment. That's what we're actually doing in meditation. Up come all these thoughts, but rather than squelch them or obsess with them, we acknowledge them and let them go. Then we come back to just being here.

After a while, that's how we relate with hope and fear in our daily lives. Out of nowhere, we stop struggling and relax. We see our story line, drop it, and come back to the freshness of the present moment.

25

Slogan: "Of the two witnesses, hold the principal one"

The main thing about bodhichitta training and about all practice is that you're the only one who knows what is opening and what is closing down. You're the only one who knows. One kind of witness is everybody else giving you his or her feedback and opinions. This is worth listening to; there's some truth in what people say. The principal witness, however, is you. You're the only one who knows when you're opening and when you're closing. You're the only one who knows when you're using things to protect yourself and keep your ego together and when you're opening and letting things fall apart, letting the world come as it is—working with it rather than struggling against it. You're the only one who knows.

Another slogan says, "Don't make gods into demons." What it means is you can take something good—mind-training practice, for example—and turn it into a demon.

You can use anything to close your windows and doors. You can use practice to bolster your sense of confidence, bolster your sense of being in the right place at the right time, of having chosen the right religion, and feeling "I'm on the side of the good and all's right with the world." That doesn't help much. Using tonglen or any practice to feel like a hero, you'll eventually come to feel like you're in a battle with reality and reality is always winning. But you're the one who knows.

26

Encountering the Edge

In the teachings of Buddhism, we hear about egoless-ness. It sounds difficult to grasp: what are they talking about, anyway? When the teachings are about neurosis we feel right at home. That's something we really understand. But egolessness? When we reach our limit, if we aspire to know that place fully—which is to say that we aspire to neither indulge nor repress—a hardness in us will dissolve. We will be softened by the sheer force of whatever energy arises—the energy of anger, the energy of disappointment, the energy of fear. When it's not solidified in one direction or another, that very energy pierces us to the heart, and it opens us. This is the discovery of egolessness. It's when all our usual schemes fall apart. Reaching our limit is like finding a doorway to sanity and the unconditional goodness of humanity, rather than meeting an obstacle or a punishment.

The safest and most nurturing place to begin working this way is during sitting meditation. On the cushion, we begin to get the hang of not indulging or repressing and of what it feels like to let the energy just be there. That is why it's so good to meditate every single day and continue to make friends with our hopes and fears again and again. This sows the seeds that enable us to be more awake in the midst of everyday chaos. It's a gradual awakening, and it's cumulative, but that's actually what happens. We don't sit in meditation to become good meditators. We sit in meditation so that we'll be more awake in our lives.

27

The Facts of Life: Suffering

The third mark of existence is suffering, dissatisfaction. To put it concisely, we suffer when we resist the noble and irrefutable truth of impermanence and death. We suffer not because we are basically bad or deserve to be punished but because of three tragic misunderstandings.

First, we expect that what is always in the process of change should be graspable and predictable. Because we mistake what is impermanent to be permanent, we suffer.

Second, we proceed as if we are separate from everything else, as if we are a fixed identity, when our true situation is egoless. Because we mistake the openness of our being for a solid, irrefutable self, we suffer.

Third, we look for happiness in all the wrong places. The Buddha called this habit "mistaking suffering for happiness." We become habituated to reaching for something to ease the edginess of the moment. Thus we become less and less able to reside with even the most fleeting uneasiness or discomfort. What begins as a slight shift of energy—a minor tightening of our stomach, a vague indefinable feeling that something bad is about to happen—escalates into addiction. This is our way of trying to make life predictable. Because we mistake what always results in suffering to be what will bring us happiness, we remain stuck in the repetitious habit of escalating our dissatisfaction.

28

Hope and Fear

One of the classic Buddhist teachings on hope and fear concerns what are known as the eight worldly dharmas. These are four pairs of opposites—four things that we like and become attached to and four things that we don't like and try to avoid. The basic message is that when we are caught up in the eight worldly dharmas, we suffer.

First, we like pleasure; we are attached to it. Conversely, we don't like pain. Second, we like and are attached to praise. We try to avoid criticism and blame. Third, we like and are attached to fame. We dislike and try to avoid disgrace. Finally, we are attached to gain, to getting what we want. We don't like losing what we have.

According to this very simple teaching, becoming immersed in these four pairs of opposites—pleasure and pain, praise and blame, fame and disgrace, and gain and loss—is what keeps us stuck in the pain of samsara.

We might feel that somehow we should try to eradicate these feelings of pleasure and pain, gain and loss, praise and blame, fame and disgrace. A more practical approach is to get to know them intimately, see how they hook us, see how they color our perception of reality, see how they aren't all that solid. Then the eight worldly dharmas become the means for growing wiser as well as kinder and more content.

29

Lighten Up
(and Do Something Different)

Being able to lighten up is the key to feeling at home with your body, mind, and emotions, to feeling worthy to live on this planet. For example, you can hear the slogan "Always maintain only a joyful mind" and start beating yourself over the head for never being joyful. That kind of witness is a bit heavy.

This earnestness, this seriousness about everything in our lives—including practice—this goal-oriented, we're-going-to-do-it-or-else attitude, is the world's greatest killjoy. There's no sense of appreciation because we're so solemn about everything. In contrast, a joyful mind is very ordinary and relaxed. So lighten up. Don't make such a big deal.

When your aspiration is to lighten up, you begin to have a sense of humor. Your serious state of mind keeps getting popped. In addition to a sense of humor, a basic support for a joyful mind is curiosity, paying attention, taking an interest in the world around you. Happiness is not required, but being curious without a heavy judgmental attitude helps. If you *are* judgmental, you can even be curious about that.

Curiosity encourages cheering up. So does simply remembering to do something different. We are so locked into this sense of burden—Big Deal Joy and Big Deal Unhappiness—that it's sometimes helpful just to change the pattern. Anything out of the ordinary will help. You can go to the window and look at the sky, you can splash cold water on your face, you can sing in the shower, you can go jogging—anything that's against your usual pattern. That's how things start to lighten up.

30

The Four Reminders

The four reminders are four good reasons why the warrior-bodhisattva makes a continual effort to return to the present moment. They are:

1. *Our precious human birth.* Just like the weather, all sorts of feelings, emotions, and thoughts come and go, but that's no reason to forget how precious the situation is. Our human birth allows us to hear these teachings, to practice, to extend our open hearts to others.

2. *The truth of impermanence.* The essence of life is fleeting. Life might be over in the next instant! Remembering impermanence can teach you a lot about how to cheer up. It's okay to let it scare you. Seeing your fear can heighten the sense of gratitude for the preciousness of human birth and the opportunity to practice.

3. *The law of karma.* Every action has a result. Every time you're willing to acknowledge your thoughts and come back to the freshness of the present moment, you're sowing seeds of wakefulness for your own future. You're cultivating innate fundamental wakefulness by aspiring to let go of the habitual way you proceed and doing something different. You're the only one who can do this. Life is precious and it's brief and you can use it well.

4. *The futility of samsara.* Samsara is preferring death to life. It comes from always trying to create safety zones. We get stuck here because we cling to a funny little identity that gives us some kind of security, painful though it may be. The fourth reminder is to remember the futility of this strategy.

31

Heaven and Hell

A big, burly samurai comes to a Zen master and says, "Tell me the nature of heaven and hell."

The Zen master looks him in the face and says, "Why should I tell a scruffy, disgusting, miserable slob like you? A worm like you, do you think I should tell you anything?"

Consumed by rage, the samurai draws his sword and raises it to cut off the master's head.

The Zen master says, "That's hell."

Instantly, the samurai understands that he has just created his own hell—black and hot, filled with hatred, self-protection, anger, and resentment. He sees that he was so deep in hell that he was ready to kill someone. Tears fill his eyes as he puts his palms together to bow in gratitude for this insight.

The Zen master says, "That's heaven."

The view of the warrior-bodhisattva is not "Hell is bad and heaven is good" or "Get rid of hell and just seek heaven." Instead, we encourage ourselves to develop an open heart and an open mind to heaven, to hell, to everything. Only with this kind of equanimity can we realize that no matter what comes along, we're always standing in the middle of a sacred space. Only with equanimity can we see that everything that comes into our circle has come to teach us what we need to know.

32

The Three Futile Strategies

There are three habitual methods that human beings use for relating to troubling habits such as laziness, anger, or self-pity. I call these the three futile strategies—the strategies of attacking, indulging, and ignoring.

The futile strategy of attacking is particularly popular. When we see our habit we condemn ourselves. We criticize and shame ourselves for indulging in comfort, or pitying ourselves, or not getting out of bed. We wallow in the feeling of badness and guilt.

The futile strategy of indulging is equally common. We justify and even applaud our habit: "This is just the way I am. I don't deserve discomfort or inconvenience. I have plenty of reasons to be angry or to sleep twenty-four hours a day." We may be haunted by self-doubt and feelings of inadequacy but we talk ourselves into condoning our behavior.

The strategy of ignoring is quite effective, at least for a while. We dissociate, space out, go numb. We do anything possible to distance ourselves from the naked truth of our habits. We go on automatic pilot and just avoid looking too closely at what we're doing.

The mind-training practices of the warrior present a fourth alternative, the alternative of an enlightened strategy. Try fully experiencing whatever you've been resisting—without exiting in your habitual ways. Become inquisitive about your habits. Practice touching in with the fundamental tenderness and groundlessness of your being before it hardens into habit. Do this with the clear intention that your ego-clinging diminish and that your wisdom and compassion increase.

33

The Opposite of Samsara

The opposite of samsara is when all the walls fall down, when the cocoon completely disappears and we are totally open to whatever may happen, with no withdrawing, no centralizing into ourselves. That is what we aspire to, the warrior's journey. That is what stirs us: leaping, being thrown out of the nest, going through the initiation rites, growing up, stepping into something that's uncertain and unknown.

What do you do when you find yourself anxious because your world is falling apart? How do you react when you're not measuring up to your image of yourself, everybody is irritating you because no one is doing what you want, and your whole life is fraught with emotional misery and confusion and conflict? At these times it helps to remember that you're going through an emotional upheaval because your coziness has just been, in some small or large way, addressed. It's as if the rug has been pulled out from under you. Tuning in to that groundless feeling is a way of remembering that basically, you *do* prefer life and warriorship to death.

34

Cultivating the Four Limitless Qualities

A teacher once told me that if I wanted lasting happiness the only way to get it was to step out of my cocoon. When I asked her how to bring happiness to others she said, "Same instruction." This is the reason that I work with the aspiration practices of the four limitless qualities of loving-kindness, compassion, joy, and equanimity: the best way to serve ourselves is to love and care for others. These are powerful tools for dissolving the barriers that perpetuate the suffering of all beings.

It is best to do sitting meditation before and after these practices. To begin, we start just where we are. We connect with the place where we currently feel loving-kindness, compassion, joy, or equanimity, however limited it may be. (You can even make a list of people or animals who inspire these feelings in you.) We aspire that ourselves and our loved ones could enjoy the quality we are practicing. Then we gradually extend that aspiration to a widening circle of relationships.

We can do these practices in three simple steps, using the words from the traditional Four Limitless Ones chant (see p. v) or whatever words make sense to us. First, we wish for ourselves one of the four limitless qualities. "May I enjoy loving-kindness." Then we include a loved one in the aspiration: "May you enjoy loving-kindness." We then extend our wish to all sentient beings: "May all beings enjoy loving-kindness." Or for compassion: "May I be free from suffering and the root of suffering. May you be free of suffering and the root of suffering. May all beings be free of suffering and the root of suffering." For a more elaborate aspiration practice, we can use seven stages (see teaching 35).

The aspiration practices of the four limitless qualities train us in not holding back, in seeing our biases and not feeding them. Gradually we will get the hang of going beyond our fear of feeling pain. This is what it takes to become involved with the sorrows of the world, to extend loving-kindness and compassion, joy and equanimity to everyone—no exceptions.

35

The Practice of Loving-Kindness

To move from aggression to unconditional loving-kindness can seem like a daunting task. But we start with what's familiar. The instruction for cultivating limitless maitri is to first find the tenderness that we already have. We touch in with our gratitude or appreciation—our current ability to feel goodwill. In a very nontheoretical way we contact the soft spot of bodhichitta. Whether we find it in the tenderness of feeling love or the vulnerability of feeling lonely is immaterial. If we look for that soft, unguarded place, we can always find it.

This formal seven-step practice uses the first line of the Four Limitless Ones chant (see page v). You can also put the aspiration in your own words.

1. Awaken loving-kindness for yourself. "May I enjoy happiness and the root of happiness," or use your own words.

2. Awaken it for someone for whom you spontaneously

feel unequivocal goodwill and tenderness, such as your mother, your child, your spouse, your dog. "May (name) enjoy happiness and the root of happiness."

3. Awaken loving-kindness for someone slightly more distant, such as a friend or neighbor, again saying their name and aspiring for their happiness, using the same words.

4. Awaken loving-kindness for someone about whom you feel neutral or indifferent, using the same words.

5. Awaken loving-kindness for someone you find difficult or offensive.

6. Let the loving-kindness grow big enough to include all the beings in the five steps above. (This step is called "dissolving the barriers.") Say, "May I, my beloved, my friend, the neutral person, the difficult person all together enjoy happiness and the root of happiness."

7. Extend loving-kindness toward all beings throughout the universe. You can start close to home and widen the circle even bigger. "May all beings enjoy happiness and the root of happiness."

At the end of the practice, drop the words, drop the wishes, and simply come back to the nonconceptual simplicity of sitting meditation.

36

Cultivating Compassion

Just as nurturing our ability to love is a way of awakening bodhichitta, so also is nurturing our ability to feel compassion. Compassion, however, is more emotionally challenging than loving-kindness because it involves the willingness to feel pain. It definitely requires the training of a warrior.

For arousing compassion, the nineteenth-century yogi Patrul Rinpoche suggests imagining beings in torment—an animal about to be slaughtered, a person awaiting execution. To make it more immediate, he recommends imagining ourselves in their place. Particularly painful is his image of a mother with no arms watching as a raging river sweeps her child away. To contact the suffering of another being fully and directly is as painful as being in that woman's shoes. For most of us, even to consider such a thing is frightening. When we practice generating compassion, we can expect to experience our fear of pain.

Compassion practice is daring. It involves learning to

relax and allowing ourselves to move gently toward what scares us. The trick to doing this is to stay with emotional distress without tightening into aversion; to let fear soften us rather than harden into resistance.

It can be difficult to even think about beings in torment, let alone to act on their behalf. Recognizing this, we begin with a practice that is fairly easy. We cultivate bravery through making aspirations. We make the wish that all beings, including ourselves and those we dislike, be free of suffering and the root of suffering.

37

The Practice of Compassion

We cultivate compassion to soften our hearts and also to become more honest and forgiving about when and how we shut down. Without justifying or condemning ourselves, we do the courageous work of opening to suffering. This can be the pain that comes when we put up barriers or the pain of opening our heart to our own sorrow or that of another being. We learn as much about doing this from our failures as we do from our successes. In cultivating compassion we draw from the wholeness of our experience—our suffering, our empathy, as well as our cruelty and terror. It has to be this way. Compassion is not a relationship between the healer and the wounded. It's a relationship between equals. Only when we know our own darkness well can we be present with the darkness of others. Compassion becomes real when we recognize our shared humanity.

As in all the aspiration practices of the four limitless qualities, we start the compassion practice where we are and then expand our capacity. We start by locating our current ability to be genuinely touched by suffering. We can make a list of those who evoke a feeling of compassion. It might include our grandchild and our brother and our friend who is afraid of dying, as well as beings we see on the news or read about in a book. The point is simply to contact genuine compassion, wherever we may find it. Then we can follow the three-step formula, "May I be free of suffering. May you be free of suffering. May we be free of suffering." We can also follow the formal seven-step process presented in teaching 35, using the words, "May I be free from suffering and the root of suffering" or the words of our choice. Like all the bodhichitta practices, the aspiration practice of compassion is best done within a session of sitting meditation.

38

Cultivating the Ability to Rejoice

As we cultivate our garden, the conditions become more conducive to the growth of bodhichitta. We begin to feel joy. It comes from not giving up on ourselves, from mindfully sticking with ourselves and beginning to experience our great warrior spirit. We also provide the conditions for joy to expand by training in the bodhichitta practices and in particular by training in rejoicing and appreciation. As with the other limitless qualities, we can do this as a three-step aspiration practice: "May I not be separated from the great happiness devoid of suffering. May you not be separated from the great happiness devoid of suffering. May we not be separated from the great happiness devoid of suffering." We can also do this as a seven-stage practice (see teaching 35). It is fine to use your own words.

The appreciation and joy in these words refer to always abiding in the wide-open, unbiased nature of our minds, to connecting with the inner strength of basic goodness. To do this, however, we start with conditioned examples of good fortune such as health, basic intelligence, a supportive environment—the fortunate conditions that constitute a precious human birth. For the awakening warrior, the greatest advantage is to find ourselves in a time when it is possible to hear and practice the bodhichitta teachings.

We can practice the first step of the aspiration by learning to rejoice in our own good fortune. The key is to be here, fully connected with the details of our lives, paying attention. We are expressing appreciation: friendship toward ourselves and toward the living quality that is found in everything. This combination of mindfulness and appreciation connects us fully with reality and brings us joy. When we extend attention and appreciation toward our environment and other people, our experience of joy expands even further.

39

The Practice of Equanimity

By practicing loving-kindness, compassion, and rejoicing, we are training in thinking bigger, in opening up as wholeheartedly as we can. We are cultivating the unbiased state of equanimity. Without this fourth boundless quality the other three are limited by our habit of liking and disliking, accepting and rejecting.

Training in equanimity is learning to open the door to all, welcoming all beings, inviting life to come visit. Of course, as certain guests arrive, we'll feel fear and aversion. We allow ourselves to open the door just a crack if that's all that we can presently do and we allow ourselves to shut the door when necessary. Cultivating equanimity is a work in progress. We aspire to spend our lives training in the loving-kindness and courage that it takes to receive whatever appears—sickness, health, poverty, wealth, sorrow, and joy. We welcome and get to know them all.

Equanimity is bigger than our usual limited perspective. It's the vast mind that doesn't narrow reality into for-or-against, liking-or-disliking. Touching in with the place where we feel equanimity, we can then formally train in cultivating it by practicing the three-step practice: "May I dwell in the great equanimity free from passion, aggression, and prejudice. May you dwell in the great equanimity free from passion, aggression, and prejudice. May all beings enjoy the great equanimity free from passion, aggression, and prejudice." It is always fine to use your own words. The aspiring practice of equanimity can also be expanded into seven stages (see teaching 35). Do some sitting meditation before and after this practice.

40

Thinking Bigger

To cultivate equanimity we practice catching ourselves when we feel attraction or aversion, before it hardens into grasping or negativity. We train in staying with the soft spot and use our biases as stepping-stones for connecting with the confusion of others. Strong emotions are useful in this regard. Whatever arises, no matter how bad it feels, can be used to extend our kinship to others who suffer the same kind of aggression or craving— who, just like us, get hooked by hope and fear. This is how we come to appreciate that everyone's in the same boat. We all desperately need more insight into what leads to happiness and what leads to pain.

It's easy to continue, even after years of practice, to harden into a position of anger and indignation. However, if we can contact the vulnerability and rawness of resentment or rage or whatever it is, a bigger perspective can emerge. In the moment that we choose to abide with the energy instead of acting it out or repressing it, we are training in equanimity, in thinking bigger than right and wrong. This is how all the four limitless qualities—love, compassion, joy, and equanimity—evolve from limited to limitless: we practice catching our mind hardening into fixed views and do our best to soften. Through softening, the barriers come down.

41

Be Where You Are

You can cultivate the four limitless qualities of love, compassion, joy, and equanimity by learning to relax where you are. There's no problem with being where you are right now. Even if you feel loving-kindness and compassion for only one sentient being, that is a good place to start. Simply acknowledging, respecting, and appreciating the warmth is a way to encourage its growth. We can be where we are and at the same time leave wide open the possibility of being able to expand far beyond where we are now in the course of our lifetime.

Expansion never happens through greediness or pushing or striving. It happens through some combination of learning to relax where you already are and, at the same time, keeping the possibility open that your capacity, my capacity, the capacity of all beings, is limitless. As we continue to relax where we are, our opening expands. This is the potential of a human being. This is the gift of a human birth. When we say, "May I have happiness," or, "May I be free of suffering," or, "May any individual have happiness and be free of suffering," we are saying that it is the potential of a human being to expand our capacity for opening and caring limitlessly. It starts out with feeling love or compassion for one being. It can expand to include more and more beings, until it reaches the full human capacity for connecting with love and compassion, which is limitless, free-flowing warmth—dynamic, alive, connected energy with no reference point. This is our human potential: to connect with the true state of affairs. It begins with being where we are.

42

Tonglen and Fearlessness

In the Buddhist teachings, in the Shambhala teachings, and in any tradition that teaches us how to live well, we are encouraged to cultivate fearlessness. How do we do that? Certainly the sitting practice of meditation is one way, because through it we come to know ourselves so completely and with such gentleness. Tonglen (sending-and-taking) practice also helps cultivate fearlessness. When you do this practice for some time, you begin to realize that fear has to do with wanting to protect your heart: you feel that something is going to harm your heart, and therefore you protect it.

After I did tonglen for the first time, I was amazed to see how I had been subtly using sitting meditation to try to avoid being hurt, to try to avoid depression, discouragement, or bad feelings of any kind. Unknown to myself, I had secretly hoped that if I did the practice I wouldn't have to feel any pain anymore. When we do tonglen, we invite the pain in. Tonglen takes courage to do, and interestingly enough, it also gives us a lot of courage, because we let it penetrate our armor. It's a practice that allows us to feel less burdened and less cramped, a practice that shows us how to love without conditions.

Negativity and resentment occur because we're trying to cover over the soft spot of bodhichitta. In fact, it's *because* we are tender and deeply touched that we do all this shielding. It's because we have this genuine heart of sadness to begin with that we even start shielding. In tonglen practice we become willing to begin to expose this most tender part of ourselves.

43

Tonglen: The Key to Realizing Interconnectedness

People generally eat up the teachings, but when it comes to doing tonglen, they say, "Oh, it sounded good, but I didn't realize you actually meant it." In its essence, this practice is: when anything is painful or undesirable, breathe it in. In other words, you don't resist it. You surrender to yourself, you acknowledge who you are, you honor yourself. As unwanted feelings and emotions arise, you actually breathe them in and connect with what all humans feel. We all know what it is to feel pain in its many guises.

You breathe in for yourself, in the sense that pain is a personal and real experience, but simultaneously there's no doubt that you're developing your kinship with all beings. If you can know it in yourself, you can know it in everyone. If you're in a jealous rage and you have the courage to breathe it in rather than blame it on someone else, the arrow you feel in your heart will tell you that there are people all over the world who are feeling exactly what you're feeling. This practice cuts through culture, economic status, intelligence, race, religion. People everywhere feel pain—jealousy, anger, being left out, feeling lonely. Everybody feels it in the painful way you feel it. The story lines vary, but the underlying feeling is the same for us all.

By the same token, if you feel some sense of delight—if you connect with what for you is inspiring, opening, relieving, relaxing—you breathe it out, you give it away, you send it out to everyone else. Again, it's very personal. It starts with *your* feeling of delight, *your* feeling of connecting with a bigger perspective, *your* feeling of relief or relaxation. If you're willing to drop the story line, you feel exactly what all other human beings feel. It's shared by all of us. In this way if we do the practice personally and genuinely, it awakens our sense of kinship with all beings.

44

The Four Stages of Tonglen

You can formally practice tonglen within a session of sitting meditation. For example, if you are sitting for an hour, you could practice tonglen during the middle twenty minutes. Tonglen practice has four stages:

1. Rest your mind for a second or two in a state of openness or stillness. This is called flashing absolute bodhichitta, or suddenly opening to the basic spaciousness and clarity of the awakened heart.

2. Work with texture. Breathe in a feeling of hot, dark, and heavy—a sense of claustrophobia—and breathe out a feeling of cool, bright, and light—a sense of freshness. Breathe in through all the pores of your body and radiate out completely, through all the pores of your body. Do this until your visualization feels synchronized with your in- and out-breaths.

3. Now contemplate any painful situation that's real to you. For example, you can breathe in the hot, dark,

constricted feeling of sadness that you feel, and breathe out a light, cool sense of joy or space or whatever might provide relief.

4. Widen the circle of compassion by connecting with all those who feel this kind of pain, and extending the wish to help everyone.

45

Start Where You Are

What we're working with in basic meditation practice—and more explicitly in tonglen practice—is the middle ground between acting out and repressing. We learn to see our thoughts of hatred, lust, poverty, loathing, whatever they might be. We learn to identify the thoughts as "thinking," let them go, and begin to contact the texture of energy that lies beneath them. We gradually begin to realize how profound it is just to let those thoughts go, not rejecting them, not repressing them. We discover how to hold our seat and feel completely what's underneath the story line of craving or aversion or jealousy or feeling wretched about ourselves, underneath all that hopelessness and despair. We can begin to feel the energy of our heart, our body, our neck, our head, our stomach—what's underneath the story lines. We find that there's something extremely soft, which is called bodhichitta. If we can relate directly with that, then all the rest is our wealth.

In postmeditation, when the poisons of passion, aggression, or ignorance arise, the instruction is to drop the story line. Instead of acting out or repressing, we use the poison as an opportunity to feel our heart, to feel the wound, and to connect with others who suffer in the same way. We can use the poison as an opportunity to contact bodhichitta. In this way, the poison already is the medicine. When we don't act out and we don't repress, our passion, our aggression, and our ignorance become our wealth. We don't have to transform anything. Simply letting go of the story line is what it takes, which is not all that easy. That light touch of acknowledging what we're thinking and letting it go is the key to touching in with the wealth of bodhichitta. With all the messy stuff, no matter how messy it is, just start where you are—not tomorrow, not later, not yesterday when you were feeling better—but now. Start now, just as you are.

46

Getting to Know Fear

We cannot be in the present moment and run our story lines at the same time. Experiment with this for yourself, and watch how it changes you. Impermanence becomes vivid in the present moment; so do compassion and wonder and courage. And so does fear. In fact, anyone who stands on the edge of the unknown, fully in the present, without a reference point, experiences ground-lessness. That's when our understanding goes deeper, when we find that the present moment is a pretty vulnerable place and that this can be completely unnerving and completely tender at the same time.

What we're talking about is getting to know fear, becoming familiar with fear, looking it right in the eye— not as a way to solve problems, but as a complete undoing of old ways of seeing, hearing, smelling, tasting, and thinking. The truth is that when we really begin to do this, we're going to be continually humbled. Fear is a natural reaction of moving closer to the truth. If we commit ourselves to staying right where we are, then our experience becomes very vivid. Things become very clear when there is nowhere to escape.

47

Recognize Suffering

Disappointment, embarrassment, and all the places where we cannot feel good are a sort of death. We've just lost our ground completely; we are unable to hold it together and feel that we're on top of things. Rather than realizing that it takes death for there to be birth, we just fight against the fear of death.

Reaching our limit is not some kind of punishment. It's actually a sign of health that when we meet the place we are about to die, we feel fear and trembling. But usually we don't take it as a message that it's time to stop struggling and look directly at what's threatening us. Things like disappointment and anxiety are messages telling us that we're about to go into unknown territory.

When we get what we don't want, when we don't get what we do want, when we become ill, when we're getting old, when we're dying—when we see any of these things in our lives—we can recognize suffering as suffering. Then we can be curious, notice, and be mindful of our reactions. Our suffering is so grounded in our fear of impermanence. Our pain is so rooted in our lopsided view of reality. Who ever got the idea that we could have pleasure without pain? It's promoted rather widely in this world, and we buy it. But pain and pleasure go together; they are inseparable. They can be celebrated. They are ordinary. Birth is painful and delightful. Death is painful and delightful. Everything that ends is also the beginning of something else. Pain is not a punishment; pleasure is not a reward.

48

Slogan: "Change your attitude, but remain natural"

The fundamental change of attitude is to breathe the undesirable in and breathe the desirable out. In contrast, the attitude that is epidemic on the planet is to push it away if it's painful and to hold on to it tightly if it's pleasant.

The basic ground of compassionate action is the importance of *working with* rather than *struggling against*. What I mean by that is working with your own unwanted, unacceptable stuff. Then when the unacceptable and unwanted appears out *there*, you relate to it based on having worked with loving-kindness for yourself. This nondualistic approach is true to the heart because it's based on our kinship with each other. We know what to say without condescension to someone else who is suffering, because we have experienced closing down, shutting off, being angry, hurt, or rebellious, and have made a relationship with those things in ourselves.

This change in attitude doesn't happen overnight; it happens gradually, at our own speed. If we have the aspiration to stop resisting those parts of ourselves that we find unacceptable and instead begin to breathe them in, this gives us much more space. We come to know every part of ourselves, with no more monsters in the closet, no more demons in the cave. We have some sense of turning on the lights and looking at ourselves honestly and with great compassion. This is the fundamental change of attitude—this working with pain and pleasure in a revolutionary and courageous way.

49

Loving-Kindness and Tonglen

The things that drive us nuts have enormous energy. That is why we fear them. For example, you are timid: you are afraid to look someone in the eye. It takes a lot of energy to maintain that. It's the way that you hold yourself together. In tonglen practice, you have the chance to own that pattern completely, not blaming anybody, and to ventilate it with the out-breath. Then you might better understand that when other people look grim, perhaps it isn't because they hate you but because they also feel timid. In this way, tonglen practice is a practice of making friends with yourself as well as a practice of compassion for others.

By practicing tonglen, you develop your sympathy for others. You begin to understand them better. Your own pain is like a stepping-stone that makes your heart bigger. It starts with creating space in which to relate directly to specific suffering—yours or someone else's. You expand the practice to understand that suffering is universal, shared by us all.

Lest we condescendingly do tonglen for the other one who's *so* confused, remember: this is a practice where compassion begins to arise because we've been in the other one's shoes. We've been angry, jealous, and lonely. We do strange things when we're in pain. Because we're lonely, we say cruel words; because we want someone to love us, we insult them. Exchanging self for other, or tonglen, begins when we can see where someone is because we've been there. It doesn't happen because we're better than they are but because human beings share the same stuff. The more we know our own, the more we're going to understand others'.

50

Slogan: "If you can practice even when distracted, you are well trained"

When the bottom is falling out we might suddenly re-call the slogan, "If you can practice even when distracted, you are well trained." If we can practice when we're jealous, resentful, scornful, when we hate ourselves, then we are well trained. Again, practice means not continuing to strengthen the habitual patterns that keep us trapped; doing anything we can to shake up and ventilate our self-justification and blame. We do our best to stay with the strong energy without acting out or repressing. In so doing, our habits become more porous.

Our patterns are, of course, well established, seductive, and comforting. Just wishing for them to be ventilated isn't enough. Mindfulness and awareness are key. Do we see the stories that we're telling ourselves and question their validity? When we are distracted by a strong emotion, do we remember that it is part of our path? Can we feel the emotion and breathe it into our hearts for ourselves and everyone else? If we can remember to experiment like this even occasionally, we are training as a warrior. And when we can't practice when distracted but *know* that we can't, we are still training well. Never underestimate the power of compassionately recognizing what's going on.

51

Deepening Tonglen

In tonglen, after genuinely connecting with the pain and your ability to open and let go, then take the practice a step further and do it for all sentient beings. This is a key point about tonglen: your own experience of pleasure and pain becomes the way that you recognize your kinship with all sentient beings. Practicing tonglen is the way you can share in the joy and the sorrow of everyone who's ever lived, everyone who's living now, and everyone who will ever live.

Whatever discomfort you feel becomes useful. "I'm miserable, I'm depressed. Okay. Let me feel it fully so that nobody else has to feel it, so that others could be free of it." It starts to awaken your heart because you have this aspiration to say, "This pain can be of benefit to others because I can be courageous enough to feel it fully so no one else has to." The joy that you feel, the sense of being able to open up and let go, also becomes a way you connect with others. On the out-breath you say, "Let me give away anything good or true that I ever feel, any sense of humor, any sense of enjoying the sun coming up and going down, any sense of delight in the world at all, so that everybody else may share in this and feel it."

If we are willing—even for one second a day—to make an aspiration to use our own pain and pleasure to help others, we are actually able to do it that much more. We can do this practice in any situation. Start with yourself. You can extend the practice to situations in which compassion spontaneously arises, exchanging yourself for someone you want to help. Then you move on to a slightly more difficult area, one in which compassion is not necessarily your first response.

52

The Empty Boat

There's a Zen story in which a man is enjoying himself on a river at dusk. He sees another boat coming down the river toward him. At first it seems so nice to him that someone else is also enjoying the river on a nice summer evening. Then he realizes that the boat is coming right toward him, faster and faster. He begins to yell, "Hey, hey, watch out! For Pete's sake, turn aside!" But the boat just comes right at him, faster and faster. By this time he's standing up in his boat, screaming and shaking his fist, and then the boat smashes right into him. He sees that it's an empty boat.

This is the classic story of our whole life situation. There are a lot of empty boats out there. We're always screaming and shaking our fists at them. Instead, we could let them stop our minds. Even if they only stop our mind for one point one seconds, we can rest in that little gap. When the story line starts, we can do the tonglen practice of exchanging ourselves for others. In this way everything we meet has the potential to help us cultivate compassion and reconnect with the spacious, open quality of our minds.

53

The Three Poisons

In the Buddhist teachings, the messy emotional stuff is called *klesha*, which means poison. There are three main poisons: passion, aggression, and ignorance. We could talk about these in different ways—for example, we could also call them craving, aversion, and couldn't care less. Addictions of all kinds come under the category of craving, which is wanting, wanting, wanting—feeling that we have to have some kind of resolution. Aversion encompasses violence, rage, hatred, and negativity of all kinds, as well as garden-variety irritation. And ignorance? Nowadays, it's usually called denial.

The three poisons are always trapping you in one way or another, imprisoning you and making your world really small. When you feel craving, you could be sitting on the edge of the Grand Canyon, but all you can see is this piece of chocolate cake that you're craving. With aversion, you're sitting on the edge of the Grand Canyon, and all you can hear is the angry words you said to someone ten years ago. With ignorance, you're sitting on the edge of the Grand Canyon with a paper bag over your head. Each of the three poisons has the power to capture you so completely that you don't even perceive what's in front of you.

The pith instruction is, whatever you do, don't try to make the poisons go away. When you're trying to make them go away, you're losing your wealth along with your neurosis. The irony is that what we most want to avoid in our lives is crucial to awakening bodhichitta. These juicy emotional spots are where a warrior gains wisdom and compassion. Of course, we'll want to get out of those spots far more often than we'll want to stay. That's why self-compassion and courage are vital. Without loving-kindness, staying with pain is just warfare.

54

On-the-Spot Tonglen

Doing tonglen throughout the day can feel more natural than doing it on the cushion. For one thing, there is never any lack of subject matter. Daily-life practice is never abstract. As soon as uncomfortable emotions come up, we train ourselves in breathing them in and dropping the story line. At the same time, we extend our thoughts and concern to other people who feel the same discomfort, and we breathe in with the wish that all of us could be free of this particular brand of confusion. Then, as we breathe out, we send ourselves and others whatever kind of relief we think would help. We also practice like this when we encounter animals and people who are in pain. We can try to do this whenever difficult situations and feelings arise. Over time it will become more automatic.

It is also helpful to notice anything in our daily life that brings us happiness. As soon as we become aware of it, we can think of sending it out to others, further cultivating the tonglen attitude.

As warrior-bodhisattvas, the more we train in cultivating this attitude, the more we uncover our capacity for joy and equanimity. Because of our bravery and willingness to work with the practice, we are more able to experience the basic goodness of ourselves and others. We're more able to appreciate the potential of all kinds of people: those we find pleasant, those we find unpleasant, and those we don't even know. Thus tonglen begins to ventilate our prejudices and introduce us to a more tender and open-minded world.

55

Start Where You Are
(Again and Again)

Start where you are. This is very important. Tonglen practice (and all meditation practice) is not about later, when you get it all together and you're this person you really respect. You may be the most violent person in the world—that's a fine place to start. That's a very rich place to start—juicy, smelly. You might be the most depressed person in the world, the most addicted person in the world, the most jealous person in the world. You might think that there are no others on the planet who hate themselves as much as you do. All of that is a good place to start. Just where you are—that's the place to start.

What you do for yourself, any gesture of kindness, any gesture of gentleness, any gesture of honesty and clear seeing toward yourself, will affect how you experience your world. In fact, it will transform how you experience the world. What you do for yourself, you're doing for others, and what you do for others, you're doing for yourself. When you exchange yourself for others in the practice of tonglen, it becomes increasingly uncertain what is out there and what is in here.

Experience Your Life

A woman is running from tigers. She runs and she runs, and the tigers are getting closer and closer. She comes to the edge of a cliff. She sees a vine there, so she climbs down and holds on to it. Then she looks down and sees that there are tigers below her as well. At the same time, she notices a little mouse gnawing away at the vine to which she is clinging. She also sees a beautiful little bunch of strawberries emerging from a nearby clump of grass. She looks up, she looks down, and she looks at the mouse. Then she picks a strawberry, pops it in her mouth, and enjoys it thoroughly.

Tigers above, tigers below. This is the predicament we are always in. We are born and sooner or later we die. Each moment is just what it is. Resentment, bitterness, and holding a grudge prevent us from seeing and hearing and tasting and delighting. This might be the only moment of our life, this might be the only strawberry we'll ever eat. We could feel depressed about this or we could finally appreciate it. We could delight in the preciousness of every single moment.

See What Is

Holding on to beliefs limits our experience of life. That doesn't mean that beliefs or opinions or ideas are a problem. It's the stubborn attitude of having to have things be a particular way, grasping on to our beliefs and opinions, that causes the problems. Using your belief system this way creates a situation in which you choose to be blind instead of being able to see, to be deaf instead of being able to hear, to be dead rather than alive, asleep rather than awake.

As people who want to live a good, full, unrestricted, adventurous, real kind of life, there is concrete instruction we can follow: see what is. When you catch yourself grasping at beliefs or thoughts, just see what is. Without calling your belief right or wrong, acknowledge it. See it clearly without judgment and let it go. Come back to the present moment. From now until the moment of your death, you could do this.

The Buddha

When people decide to become Buddhists, they participate in an official ceremony in which they take refuge in the three jewels—the Buddha, the dharma, and the sangha. I've always thought it sounds theistic, dualistic, and dependent "to take refuge" in something. However, the fundamental idea of taking refuge is that between birth and death we are alone. Therefore taking refuge in the three jewels doesn't mean finding consolation in them. Rather, it's a basic expression of our aspiration to leap out of the nest, whether we feel ready for it or not, to go through our puberty rites and be an adult with no hand to hold. Taking refuge is the way that we begin cultivating the openness and the good-heartedness that allow us to be less and less dependent.

The Buddha is the awakened one, and we too are buddhas. We are the awakened one—the one who continually leaps, who continually opens, who continually goes forward. Being a buddha isn't easy. It's accompanied by fear, resentment, and doubt. But learning to leap into open space with our fear, resentment, and doubt is how we become fully human beings. There isn't any separation between samsara and nirvana, between the sadness and pain of the setting sun and the vision and power of the Great Eastern Sun, as the Shambhala teachings put it. One can hold them both in one's heart, which is actually the purpose of practice.

Taking refuge in the Buddha means that we are willing to spend our life reconnecting with the quality of being continually awake. Every time we feel like taking refuge in a habitual means of escape, we take off more armor, undoing all the stuff that covers over our wisdom and our gentleness and our awake quality. We're not trying to be something we aren't; rather, we're reconnecting with who we are. So when we say, "I take refuge in the Buddha," that means I take refuge in the courage and the potential of fearlessness, of removing all the armor that covers this awakeness of mine. I am awake; I will spend my life taking this armor off. Nobody else can take if off because nobody else knows where all the little locks are, nobody else knows where it's sewed up tight, where it's going to take a lot of work to get that particular iron thread untied. You have to do it alone. The basic instruction is simple: Start taking off that armor. That's all anyone can tell you. No one can tell you how to do it because you're the only one who knows how you locked yourself in there to start.

59

Nowness

There was once a lady who was arrogant and proud. Determined to attain enlightenment, she asked all the authorities how to go about it. She was told, "Well, if you climb to the top of this very high mountain, you'll find a cave there. Sitting inside that cave is a wise old woman. She will tell you."

Having endured great hardships, the lady finally found this cave. Sure enough, sitting there was a gentle, spiritual-looking old woman in white clothing who smiled beatifically. Overcome with awe and respect, the lady prostrated at the feet of this woman and said, "I want to attain enlightenment. Show me how." The wise woman looked at her and asked sweetly, "Are you sure you want to attain enlightenment?" And the woman said, "Of course I'm sure." Whereupon the smiling woman turned into a demon, stood up brandishing a great big stick, and started chasing her, saying, "Now! Now! Now!" For the rest of her life, that lady could never get away from the demon who was always saying, "Now!"

Now—that's the key. Mindfulness trains us to be awake and alive, fully curious, about *now*. The out-breath is *now*, the in-breath is *now*, waking up from our fantasies is *now*, and even the fantasies are *now*. The more you can be completely *now*, the more you realize that you're always standing in the middle of a sacred circle. It's no small affair, whether you're brushing your teeth or cooling your food or wiping your bottom. Whatever you're doing, you're doing it now.

60

The Heart of Everyday Life

The Buddha said that we are never separated from enlightenment. Even at the times we feel most stuck, we are never alienated from the awakened state. This is a revolutionary assertion. Even ordinary people like us with hang-ups and confusion have this mind of enlightenment called bodhichitta. An analogy for bodhichitta is the rawness of a broken heart. This is our link with all those who have ever loved. This genuine heart of sadness can teach us great compassion. It can humble us when we're arrogant and soften us when we are unkind. It awakens us when we prefer to sleep and pierces through our indifference. This continual ache of the heart broken open is a blessing that when accepted fully can be shared with all.

The openness and warmth of bodhichitta is in fact our true nature and condition. Even when our neurosis feels far more basic than our wisdom, even when we're feeling most confused and hopeless, bodhichitta—like the open sky—is always here, undiminished by the clouds that temporarily cover it.

Bodhichitta is available in moments of caring for things, when we clean our glasses or brush our hair. It's available in moments of appreciation, when we notice the blue sky or pause and listen to the rain. It's available in moments of gratitude, when we recall a kindness or recognize another person's courage. It's available in music and dance, in art, and in poetry. Whenever we let go of holding on to ourselves and look at the world around us, whenever we connect with sorrow, whenever we connect with joy, whenever we drop our resentment and complaint, in those moments bodhichitta is here.

61

Widening the Circle of Compassion

It's daring not to shut anyone out of our hearts, not to make anyone an enemy. If we begin to live like this, we'll find that we actually can't define someone as completely right or completely wrong anymore. Life is more slippery and playful than that. Trying to find absolute rights and wrongs is a trick we play on ourselves to feel secure and comfortable.

Compassionate action, being there for others, being able to act and speak in a way that communicates, begins with noticing when we start to make ourselves right or make ourselves wrong. At that particular point, we could just contemplate the fact that there is an alternative to either of those, which is bodhichitta. This tender shaky place, if we can touch it, will help us train in opening further to whatever we feel, to open further rather than shut down more. We'll find that as we begin to commit ourselves to the practice of tonglen, as we begin to celebrate aspects of ourselves that we found so impossible before, something will shift permanently in us. Our ancient habitual patterns will begin to soften, and we'll begin to see the faces and hear the words of people who are talking to us. As we learn to have compassion for ourselves, the circle of compassion—what and whom we can work with, and how—expands.

62

Inconvenience

When you start to take the warrior's journey, you're going to find that it's often extremely inconvenient. When you start to want to live your life fully instead of opting for death, you discover that life itself is inconvenient. Wholeheartedness is a precious gift, but no one can actually give it to you. You have to find the path that has heart and then walk it impeccably. In doing that, you again and again encounter the inconvenience of your own uptightness, your own headaches, your own falling flat on your face. But in wholeheartedly practicing and wholeheartedly following the path, this inconvenience is not an obstacle. It's simply a certain texture of life, a certain energy of life.

Not only that, sometimes when you just get flying and it all feels so good and you think, "This is it, this is that path that has heart," you suddenly fall flat on your face. Everybody's looking at you. You say to yourself, "What happened to that path that had heart? This feels like the path full of mud in my face." Since you are wholeheart-edly committed to the warrior's journey, it pricks you, it pokes you. It's like someone laughing in your ear, chal-lenging you to figure out what to do when you don't know what to do. It humbles you. It opens your heart.

63

Widening the Circle Further

How is there going to be less aggression on the planet rather than more? Bring this question down to a personal level: How do I learn to communicate with somebody who is hurting me or hurting others? How do I communicate so that the space opens up and both of us begin to touch in to some kind of basic intelligence that we all share? How do I communicate so that things that seem frozen, unworkable, and eternally aggressive begin to soften up and some kind of compassionate exchange begins to happen?

Begin with being willing to feel what you are going through. Be willing to have a compassionate relationship with the parts of yourself that you feel are not worthy of existing. If you are willing through meditation to be mindful not only of what feels comfortable but also of what pain feels like, if you even *aspire* to stay awake and open to what you're feeling, to recognize and acknowledge it as best you can in each moment, then something begins to change.

64

What Is Karma?

Karma is a difficult subject. Basically it means that what happens in your life is somehow a result of things that you have done before. That's why you are encouraged to work with what happens to you rather than blame it on others. This kind of teaching on karma can easily be misunderstood. People get into a heavy-duty sin-and-guilt trip. They feel that if things are going wrong, it means they did something bad and they're being punished. But that's not the idea at all. The idea of karma is that you continually get the teachings you need in order to open your heart. To the degree that you didn't understand in the past how to stop protecting your soft spot, how to stop armoring your heart, now you're given this gift of teachings in the form of your life. Your life gives you everything you need to learn how to open further.

65

Growing Up

Learning how to be kind to ourselves is important. When we look into our own hearts and begin to discover what is confused and what is brilliant, what is bitter and what is sweet, it isn't just ourselves that we're discovering. We're discovering the universe. When we discover the buddha that we are, we realize that everything and everyone is buddha. We discover that everything is awake, and everyone is awake. Everything and everyone is precious and whole and good. When we regard thoughts and emotions with humor and openness, that's how we perceive the universe.

This opening to the world begins to benefit ourselves and others simultaneously. The more we relate with others, the more quickly we discover where we're blocked. Seeing this is helpful, but it's also painful. Sometimes we use it as ammunition against ourselves: we aren't kind, we aren't honest, we aren't brave, and we might as well give up right now. But when we apply the instruction to be soft and nonjudgmental to whatever we see at this very moment, the embarrassing reflection in the mirror becomes our friend. We soften further and lighten up more, because we know it's the only way we can continue to work with others and be of any benefit in the world. This is the beginning of growing up.

66

Slogan: "Don't expect applause"

What this slogan means is don't expect thanks. This is important. When you open the door and invite all sentient beings as your guests—and you also open the windows and the walls even start falling down—you find yourself in the universe with no protection at all. Now you're in for it. If you think that just by doing that you are going to feel good about yourself and you are going to be thanked right and left—no, that won't happen. More than to expect thanks, it would be helpful just to expect the unexpected; then you might be curious and inquisitive about what comes in the door. We can begin to open our hearts to others when we have no hope of getting anything back. We just do it for its own sake.

On the other hand, it's good to express our gratitude to others. It's helpful to express our appreciation of others. But if we do that with the motivation of wanting them to like us, we can remember this slogan. We can thank others, but we should give up all hope of getting thanked in return. Simply keep the door open without expectations.

67

Six Ways of Compassionate Living

There are six traditional activities in which the bodhisattva trains, six ways of compassionate living: generosity, discipline, patience, joyful exertion, meditation, and prajna, unconditional wisdom. Traditionally these are called the *paramitas*, a Sanskrit word meaning "gone to the other shore." Each one is an activity we can use to take us beyond aversion and attachment, beyond being all caught up in ourselves, beyond our illusion of separateness. Each paramita has the ability to take us beyond our fear of letting go. Through paramita training we learn to be comfortable with uncertainty. Going to the other shore has a groundless quality, a sense of being caught in the middle, being caught in the in-between state.

It is easy to regard the paramitas as a rigid code of ethics, a list of rules. But the warrior-bodhisattva's world is not that simple. The power of these activities is not that they are commandments, but that they challenge our habitual reactions. Paramita training has a way of humbling us and keeping us honest. When we practice generosity we become intimate with our grasping. Practicing the discipline of not causing harm, we see our rigidity and desire to control. Practicing patience helps us train in abiding with the restlessness of our energy and letting things evolve at their own speed. In joyful exertion we let go of our perfectionism and connect with the living quality of every moment. Meditation is how we train in coming back to being right here. And the inquiring mind of prajna—seeing things just as they are—is the key to this training, because without prajnaparamita, or unconditional bodhichitta, the other five activities can be used to give us the illusion of gaining ground.

68

Prajna

Prajna is the wisdom that cuts through the immense suffering that comes from seeking to protect our own territory. Prajna makes it impossible for us to use our actions as ways of becoming secure. Prajna turns all actions into gold. It is said that the other five transcendent activities—generosity, discipline, exertion, patience, and meditation—could give us reference points, but prajna cuts through the whole thing. Prajna makes us homeless; we have no place to dwell on anything. Because of this, we can finally relax.

Sometimes we feel tremendous longing for our old habits. When we work with generosity, we see our nostalgia for wanting to hold on. Working with discipline, we see our nostalgia for wanting to zone out and not relate at all. As we work with patience, we discover our longing to speed. When we practice exertion, we realize our laziness. With meditation we see our endless discursiveness, our restlessness, and our attitude of "couldn't care less."

Because of prajna, these other five actions, or paramitas, become the means of shedding our defenses. Every time we give, every time we practice discipline, patience, or exertion, it's like putting down a heavy burden. The foundation of the prajnaparamita is mindfulness, an open-ended inquiry into our experience. We question without the intention of finding permanent solutions. We cultivate a mind that is ready and inquisitive, not satisfied with limited or biased views. With this unfixated mind of prajna we practice the other paramitas, moving from narrow-mindedness to flexibility and fearlessness.

69

Generosity

The essence of generosity is letting go. Pain is always a sign that we are holding on to something—usually ourselves. When we feel unhappy, when we feel inadequate, we get stingy; we hold on tight. Generosity is an activity that loosens us up. By offering whatever we can—a dollar, a flower, a word of encouragement—we are training in letting go.

There are so many ways to practice generosity. The main point isn't so much what we give, but that we unlock our habit of clinging. A traditional practice is simply to offer an object that we cherish from one hand to the other. A woman I know decided that whatever she was attached to she'd give away. One man gave money to people begging in the streets every day for six months after the death of his father. It was his way of working with grief. Another woman trained in visualizing giving away whatever she most feared losing.

Giving practice shows us where we're holding back,

where we're still clinging. We start with our well-laid plans, but life blows them apart. From a gesture of generosity, true letting go will evolve. Our conventional perspective will begin to change. The causes of aggression and fear begin to dissolve by themselves when we move past the poverty of holding back and holding on.

The journey of generosity is one of connecting with the wealth of bodhichitta so profoundly that we are willing to begin to give away whatever blocks it. We open ourselves and let ourselves be touched. We build confidence in all-pervasive richness. At the everyday level, we experience it as flexibility and warmth.

70

Discipline

Dissolving the causes of aggression takes discipline, gentle yet precise discipline. Without the paramita of discipline, we simply don't have the support we need to evolve. At the outer level, we could think of discipline as a structure, like a thirty-minute meditation period or a two-hour class on the dharma. Probably the best example is the meditation technique. We sit down in a certain position and are as faithful to the technique as possible. We simply put light attention on the out-breath over and over through mood swings, through memories, through dramas and boredom. This simple repetitive process is like inviting that basic richness into our lives. So we follow the instruction just as centuries of meditators have done before.

Within this structure, we proceed with compassion. On the inner level, the discipline is to return to gentleness, to honesty, to letting go. The discipline is to find the balance between not too tight and not too loose— between not too laid-back and not too rigid.

Discipline provides us with the support to slow down enough and to be present enough so that we can live our lives without making a mess. It provides the encouragement to step further into groundlessness. We are disciplining any form of potential escape from reality. Discipline allows us to be right here and connect with the richness of the moment.

71

Patience

The power of the paramita of patience is that it is the antidote to anger, a way to learn to love and care for whatever we meet on the path. By patience, we do not mean enduring—grin and bear it. In any situation, instead of reacting suddenly, we could chew it, smell it, look at it, and open ourselves to seeing what's there. The opposite of patience is aggression—the desire to jump and move, to push against our lives, to try to fill up space. The journey of patience involves relaxing, opening to what's happening, experiencing a sense of wonder.

One of the ways to practice patience is to do tonglen. When we want to make a sudden move, when we start to speed through life, when we feel we must have resolution, when someone yells at us and we feel insulted, we want to yell back or get even. We want to put out our poison. Instead, we can connect with basic human restlessness, basic human aggression, by practicing tonglen for all beings. Then we can send out a sense of space, which further slows things down. Sitting there, standing there, we can allow the space for the usual habitual thing *not* to happen. Our words and actions might be quite different because we allowed ourselves time to touch and taste and see the situation first.

As we train in the paramita of patience, we are first of all patient with ourselves. We learn to relax with the restlessness of our energy—the energy of anger, boredom, and excitement. Patience takes courage. It is not an ideal state of calm. In fact, when we practice patience we will see our agitation far more clearly.

72

Joyous Exertion

The paramita of exertion is connected with joy. In practicing this paramita, like little children learning to walk, we train with eagerness but without a goal. This joyful uplifted energy isn't a matter of luck. It takes ongoing training in mindfulness and maitri, in dissolving the barriers and opening the heart. As we learn to relax with groundlessness, this enthusiasm will emerge.

Through continual practice we find out how to cross over the boundary between being stuck and waking up. It depends on our willingness to experience directly feelings we've been avoiding for many years. This willingness to stay open to what scares us weakens our habits of avoidance. It's the way that ego-clinging becomes ventilated and begins to fade.

The more we connect with a bigger perspective, the more we connect with energetic joy. Exertion is connecting with our appetite for enlightenment. It allows us to act, to give, to work appreciatively with whatever comes our way. If we really knew how unhappy it was making this whole planet that we all try to avoid pain and seek pleasure—how that is making us so miserable and cutting us off from our basic goodness—then we would practice as if our hair were on fire. There wouldn't be any question of thinking we have a lot of time and we can do this later.

Yet when we begin to practice exertion, we see that sometimes we can do it and sometimes we can't. The question becomes: How do we connect with inspiration? How do we connect with the spark and joy that's available in every moment?

73

Meditation

When we sit down to meditate we leave behind the idea of the perfect meditator, the ideal meditation, and preconceived results. We train in simply being present. We open ourselves completely to the pain and the pleasure of our life. We train in precision, gentleness, and letting go. Because we see our thoughts and emotions with compassion, we stop struggling against ourselves. We learn to recognize when we're all caught up and to trust that we can let go. Thus the blockages created by our habits and prejudices start falling apart. In this way, the wisdom we were blocking—the wisdom of bodhichitta—becomes available.

Meditation may be the only thing we do that doesn't add anything to the picture. When we sit down to meditate, we can connect with something unconditional—a state of mind, a basic environment that doesn't grasp or reject. Everything is allowed to come and go without further embellishment. Meditation is a totally nonviolent, nonaggressive occupation. Not filling the space, allowing for the possibility of connecting with unconditional openness—this provides the basis for real change. The more we sit with this impossibility, the more we find it's always possible after all.

When we cling to thoughts and memories, we are clinging to what cannot be grasped. When we touch these phantoms and let them go, we may discover a space, a break in the chatter, a glimpse of open sky. This is our birthright—the wisdom with which we were born, the vast unfolding display of primordial richness, primordial openness, primordial wisdom itself. When one thought has ended and another has not yet begun, we can rest in that space.

74

Letting the World Speak for Itself ("Don't Misinterpret")

The slogan "Don't misinterpret" means don't impose the wrong notion of what harmony is, what compassion is, what patience is, what generosity is. Don't misinterpret what these things really are. There is compassion and there is idiot compassion; there is patience and there is idiot patience; there is generosity and there is idiot generosity. For example, trying to smooth everything out to avoid confrontation, to not rock the boat, is not what's meant by compassion or patience. That's what is meant by control. Then you are not trying to step into unknown territory, to find yourself more naked with less protection and therefore more in contact with reality. Instead, you use the idiot forms of compassion and so forth just to get ground.

When you open the door and invite in all sentient beings as your guests, you have to drop your agenda. Many different people come in. Just when you think you have a little scheme that is going to work, it doesn't work. It was very beneficial to one person, but when you try it on the next person, he looks at you as if you're crazy, and when you try it on somebody else, she gets insulted. Coming up with a formula won't work. You don't know what's going to help, but all the same you need to speak and act with clarity and decisiveness. Clarity and decisiveness come from the willingness to slow down, to listen to and look at what's happening. They come from opening your heart and not running away. Then your actions and speech accord with what needs to be done—for you and for the other person.

75

Meditation and Prajna

As human beings, not only do we seek resolution, we feel that we deserve resolution. However, not only do we not deserve resolution, we suffer from resolution. We deserve something better than resolution: we deserve our birthright, which is prajna, an open state of mind that can relax with paradox and ambiguity.

Prajna is the unfiltered expression of the open ear, open eye, open mind that is found in every living being. It's a fluid process, not something definite and concrete that can be summed up or measured.

Prajnaparamita is our human experience. It is not particularly regarded as a peaceful state of mind nor as a disturbed one. It is a state of basic intelligence that is open, questioning, and unbiased. Whether it comes in the form of curiosity, bewilderment, shock, or relaxation isn't really the issue. We train when we're caught off guard and when our life is up in the air.

Meditation provides a way for us to train in prajna—

in staying open right on the spot. We train, as Trungpa Rinpoche said, in "not afraid to be a fool." We cultivate a simple direct relationship with our being—no philosophizing, no moralizing, no judgments. Whatever arises in our mind is workable.

It's like lying in bed before dawn and hearing rain on the roof. This simple sound can be disappointing because we were planning a picnic. It can be pleasing because our garden is so dry. But the flexible mind of prajna doesn't draw conclusions of good or bad. It perceives the sound without adding anything extra, without judgments of happy or sad.

76

Plan to Stay Open

At the beginning of your day, using your own language, encourage yourself to keep your heart open, to remain curious, no matter how difficult things get. Then at the end of the day when you're just about to go to sleep, review what happened. You may notice that the whole day went by and you never once remembered what you had aspired to do in the morning. Rather than using that as ammunition for feeling bad about yourself, use it as an opportunity to get to know yourself better. Use it to see all the funny ways in which you trick yourself, all the ways in which you're so good at zoning out and shutting down. If you don't want to do the bodhichitta practices anymore because it feels like a set-up for failure, generate a kind heart toward yourself. Reflecting over just one day's activities can be painful, but you may end up respecting yourself more. You'll see that there are many changes in the weather of a day; we're never just one way or another. The more you're willing to open your heart, the more challenges come along.

77

Slogan: "Abandon any hope of fruition"

"Fruition" implies that at some future time you will feel good. One of the most powerful Buddhist teachings is that as long as you are wishing for things to change, they never will. As long as you're wanting yourself to get better, you won't. As long as you are oriented toward the future, you can never just relax into what you already have or already are.

One of the deepest habitual patterns that we have is the feeling that the present moment is not good enough. We frequently think back to the past, which maybe was better than now, or perhaps worse. We also think ahead quite a bit to the future, always holding out hope that it will be a little bit better than now. Even if things are going really well now, we usually don't give ourselves full credit for who we are in the present.

For example, it's easy to hope that things will improve as a result of meditation: we won't have such a bad temper anymore or we won't be afraid anymore or people will like us more than they do now. Or perhaps we will fully connect with that awake, brilliant, sacred world that we hope to find. We use our practice to reinforce the implication that if we just did the right things, we'd begin to connect with a bigger world, a vaster world, a world different from the one we're in now.

Instead of looking for fruition, we could just try to stay with our open heart and open mind. This is very much oriented to the present. By entering into this kind of unconditional relationship with ourselves, we can begin to connect with the awake quality that we already have.

Right now, can you make an unconditional relationship with yourself? Just at the height you are, the weight you are, with the intelligence that you have, and your current burden of pain? Can you enter into an unconditional relationship with that?

78

Cool Loneliness

Cool loneliness allows us to look honestly and without aggression at our own minds. We can gradually drop our ideas of who we think we ought to be, or who we think we want to be, or who we think other people think we want to be or ought to be. We give it up and just look directly with compassion and humor at who we are. Then loneliness is no threat and heartache, no punishment.

Cool loneliness doesn't provide any resolution or give us ground under our feet. It challenges us to step into a world of no reference point without polarizing or solidifying. This is called the middle way, which is another way of describing the path of the warrior-bodhisattva.

When you wake up in the morning and out of nowhere comes the heartache of alienation and loneliness, could you use that as a golden opportunity? Rather than persecuting yourself or feeling that something terribly wrong is happening, right there in the moment of sadness and longing, could you relax and touch the limitless space of the human heart? The next time you get a chance, experiment with this.

79

Slogan: *"Practice the three difficulties"*

The three difficulties are acknowledging neurosis as neurosis, doing something different, and aspiring to continue practicing this way.

Acknowledging that we are all churned up is the first and most difficult step. Without recognition that we're stuck, it's impossible to liberate ourselves from confusion. "Doing something different" is anything that interrupts our strong tendency to spin out. We can let the story line go and connect with the underlying energy, do on-the-spot tonglen, remember a slogan, or burst into song—anything that doesn't reinforce our crippling habits. The third difficult practice is to then remember that we need to keep doing the first two. Interrupting our destructive habits and awakening our heart is the work of a lifetime.

In essence the practice is always the same: instead of falling prey to a chain reaction of revenge or self-hatred, we gradually learn to catch the emotional reaction and drop the story lines. Then we feel the bodily sensation completely. One way of doing this is to breathe it into our heart. By acknowledging the emotion, dropping whatever story we are telling ourselves about it, and feeling the energy of the moment, we cultivate maitri and compassion for ourselves. Then we could recognize that there are millions who are feeling the way we do and breathe in the emotion for all of us with the wish that we all be free of confusion and limiting habitual reactions. When we can recognize our own confusion with compassion, we can extend that compassion to others who are equally confused. In this step of widening the circle of compassion lies the magic of bodhichitta training.

80

Communicating from the Heart

We have a strong tendency to distance ourselves from our experience because it hurts, but the dharma provides encouragement to move closer to that experience. Although there are lots of words that could be used to explain compassionate action, I'd like to stress the word *communication*—in particular, communication from the heart.

All activities should be done with the intention of communicating. This is a practical suggestion: all activities should be done with the intention of speaking so that another person can hear you, rather than using words that cause the barriers to go up and the ears to close. In this process we also learn how to listen and how to look. You can practice making your actions, your speech, and your thoughts inseparable from this yearning to communicate from the heart. Everything you say can further polarize the situation and convince you of how separate you are. On the other hand, everything you say and do and think can support your desire to communicate, to move closer and step out of this myth of isolation and separateness that we're all caught in.

Taking this kind of responsibility is another way of talking about awakening bodhichitta, because part of taking responsibility is the quality of being able to see things very clearly. Another part of taking responsibility is gentleness, which goes along with not judging but rather looking gently and honestly at yourself. There is also the ability to keep going forward. You can just keep on going; you don't have to get frozen in an identity as a loser or a winner, the abuser or the abused, the good guy or the bad guy. You just see what you do as clearly and as compassionately as you can and then go on. The next moment is always fresh and open.

81

The Big Squeeze

If we want to communicate and we have a strong aspiration to help others—in terms of engaging in social action, helping our family or community, or just being there for people when they need us—then sooner or later we're going to experience the big squeeze. Our ideals and the reality of what's happening don't match. We feel as if we're between the fingers of a big giant who is squeezing us. We find ourselves between a rock and a hard place.

There is often a discrepancy between our ideals and what we actually encounter. For instance, in raising children, we have a lot of good ideas, but sometimes it's challenging to put together the good ideas with how our children are, there at the breakfast table with food all over themselves. Or in meditation, have you noticed how difficult it is to feel emotions without getting totally swept away by them, or how difficult it is simply to cultivate friendliness toward yourself when you're feeling miserable or panicked or all caught up?

There's a discrepancy between our inspiration and the situation as it presents itself. It's the rub between those two things—the squeeze between reality and vision—that causes us to grow up, to wake up to be 100 percent decent, alive, and compassionate. The big squeeze is one of the most productive places on the spiritual path and in particular on this journey of awakening the heart.

82

Curiosity and the Circle of Compassion

The tendency to centralize into ourselves, to try to protect ourselves, is strong and all-pervasive. A simple way of turning it around is to develop our curiosity and our inquisitiveness about everything. This is another way of talking about helping others, but of course the process also helps us. We work on ourselves in order to help others, but also we help others in order to work on ourselves. The whole path seems to be about developing curiosity, about looking out and taking an interest in all the details of our lives and in our immediate environment.

When we find ourselves in a situation in which our buttons are being pushed, we can choose to repress or act out, or we can choose to practice. If we can start to practice tonglen on the spot, breathing in with the intention of keeping our hearts open to the embarrassment or fear or anger that we feel, then to our surprise we find that we're also open to what the other person is feeling. Open heart is open heart. Once it's open, your eyes and your mind are also open, and you can see what's happening in the faces and hearts of other people. If you're walking down the street and far in the distance—so far that you can't possibly do anything about it—you see a man beating his dog, then you can do tonglen for the dog and the man. At the same time, you're doing it for your own heartbreak, for all the animals and people who are abusing and abused, and for all the people like you who are watching and don't know what to do. Simply by doing this exchange you have made the world a larger, more loving place.

83

Take Tonglen Further

In the practice of awakening our hearts, the circle of compassion widens at its own speed and widens spontaneously. It's not something you can make happen. It's definitely not something you can fake. But you can encourage yourself to at least experiment with faking it occasionally by seeing what happens when you try to do tonglen for your enemy. Try this when your enemy is standing in front of you or when you're intentionally bringing up the memory of your enemy in order to do tonglen. Think of this simple instruction: what would it take to be able to have my enemy hear what I'm trying to say, and what would it take for me to be able to hear what he or she is trying to say to me? How to communicate from the heart is the essence of tonglen.

Doing tonglen for all sentient beings doesn't have to be separate from doing it for yourself and your immediate situation. That's a point we need to hear again and again. When you connect with your own suffering, reflect that countless beings at this very moment are feeling exactly what you feel. Their story lines are different but the feeling of pain is the same. When you do the practice for all sentient beings and for yourself at the same time, you begin to realize that self and other are not actually different.

84

Slogan: "Be grateful to everyone"

"Be grateful to everyone" is about making peace with the aspects of ourselves that we have rejected. Through doing that, we also make peace with the people we dislike. More to the point, being around people we dislike can be a catalyst for making friends with ourselves.

If we were to make a list of people we don't like—people we find obnoxious, threatening, or worthy of contempt—we would discover much about those aspects of ourselves that we can't face. If we were to come up with one word about each of the troublemakers in our lives, we would find ourselves with a list of descriptions of our own rejected qualities. We project these onto the outside world. The people who repel us unwittingly show us aspects of ourselves that we find unacceptable, which otherwise we can't see. Traditional lojong teachings say it another way: other people trigger the karma that we haven't worked out. They mirror us and give us the chance to befriend all of that ancient stuff that we carry around like a backpack full of granite boulders.

"Be grateful to everyone" is a way of saying that we can learn from any situation, especially if we practice this slogan with awareness. The people and situations in our lives can remind us to catch neurosis as neurosis—to see when we've pulled the shades, locked the door, and crawled under the covers.

85

Obstacles as Questions

Obstacles occur at the outer and inner levels. At the outer level the sense is that something or somebody has harmed us, interfering with the harmony and peace we thought was ours. Some rascal has ruined it all. This particular sense of obstacle occurs in relationships and in many other situations; we feel disappointed, harmed, confused, and attacked in a variety of ways. People have felt this way from the beginning of time.

As for the inner level of obstacle, perhaps nothing ever really attacks us except our own confusion. Perhaps there is no solid obstacle except our own need to protect ourselves from being touched. Maybe the only enemy is that we don't like the way reality is *now* and therefore wish it would go away fast. But what we find as practitioners is that nothing ever goes away until it has taught us what we need to know. Even if we run a hundred miles an hour to the other side of the continent, we find the very same problem awaiting us when we arrive. It keeps returning with new names, forms, and manifestations until we learn whatever it has to teach us: Where are we separating ourselves from reality? How are we pulling back instead of opening up? How are we closing down instead of allowing ourselves to experience fully whatever we encounter?

86

Six Ways to Be Lonely

Usually we regard loneliness as an enemy. It's restless and pregnant and hot with the desire to escape and find something or someone to keep us company. When we rest in the middle of it, we begin to have a nonthreatening relationship with loneliness, a cooling loneliness that turns our usual fearful patterns upside down. There are six ways of describing this kind of cool loneliness:

1. *Less desire* is the willingness to be lonely without resolution when everything in us yearns for something to change our mood.

2. *Contentment* means that we no longer believe that escaping our loneliness is going to bring happiness or courage or strength.

3. *Avoiding unnecessary activities* means that we stop looking for something to entertain us or to save us.

4. *Complete discipline* means that at every opportunity,

we're willing to come back to the present moment with compassionate attention.

5. *Not wandering in the world of desire* is about relating directly with how things are, without trying to make them okay.

6. *Not seeking security from one's discursive thoughts* means no longer seeking the companionship of constant conversation with ourselves.

87

Thoroughly Processed

Understanding how our emotions have the power to run us around in circles helps us discover how we increase our pain, how we increase our confusion, how we cause harm to ourselves. Because we have basic goodness, basic wisdom, basic intelligence, we can stop harming ourselves and harming others.

Because of mindfulness, we see things when they arise. Because of our understanding, we don't buy into the chain reaction that makes things grow from minute to expansive—we leave things minute. They don't keep expanding into World War III or domestic violence. It all comes through learning to pause for just a moment and not doing the same thing again and again out of impulse. Simply to pause instead of immediately filling up the space transforms us. By waiting, we begin to connect with fundamental restlessness as well as fundamental spaciousness.

The result is that we cease to cause harm. We begin to know ourselves thoroughly and to respect ourselves and others. Anything can come up, anything can walk into our house. We can find a dinosaur sitting on our living room couch, and we don't freak out. We have been thoroughly processed by coming to know ourselves with honest, gentle mindfulness.

88

Commitment

Recently I taught a weekend program in a kind of New Age spiritual shopping mart. Mine was one of about seventy different workshops being presented. The people in the parking lot or at lunch would say to each other, "Oh, what are you taking this weekend?" I hadn't encountered anything like that for a long time.

Once I was shopping around for a spiritual path myself. In order to stop, I had to hear my teacher Chögyam Trungpa say that shopping around is an attempt to find security, an attempt to find a way to always feel good about yourself. You can hear the dharma from many different places, but you are uncommitted until you encounter a particular way that rings true in your heart and you decide to follow it. In order to go deeper, there has to be a wholehearted commitment. You begin the warrior's journey when you choose one path and stick to it. Then you let it put you through your changes. Without a commitment, the minute you really begin to hurt, you'll just leave or you'll look for something else.

The question always remains: To what are we really committed? Is it to playing it safe and manipulating our life and the rest of the world so that it will give us security and confirmation? Or is our commitment to exploring deeper and deeper levels of letting go? Do we take refuge in small, self-satisfied actions, speech, and mind? Or do we take refuge in warriorship, in taking a leap, in going beyond our usual safety zones?

89

Three Methods for Working
with Chaos

There are three very practical ways for relating with difficult circumstances as the path of awakening and joy: no more struggle, poison as medicine, and regarding everything that arises as the manifestation of wisdom.

The first method is epitomized by meditation instruction. Whatever arises in our minds we look at directly, call it "thinking," and go back to the simplicity and immediacy of the breath. When we encounter difficulties in our lives, we can continue to train in this way. We can drop the story line, slow down enough to just be present, let go of the multitude of judgments and schemes, and stop struggling.

Second, we can use poison as fuel for waking up. In general, this idea is introduced to us with tonglen. Instead of pushing difficult situations away, we can use them to connect with other people who, just like us, often find themselves in pain. As one slogan puts it,

"When the world is filled with evil, transform all mishaps into the path of enlightenment."

The third method for working with chaos is to regard whatever arises as the manifestation of awakened energy. We can regard ourselves as already awake; we can regard our world as already sacred. This view further encourages us to use everything in our lives as the basis for attaining enlightenment.

The world we find ourselves in, the person we think we are—these are our working bases. This charnel ground called life is the manifestation of wisdom. This wisdom is the basis of freedom and also the basis of confusion. In every moment, we make a choice: Which way do we go? How do we relate with the raw material of our existence?

90

On-the-Spot Equanimity

An on-the-spot equanimity practice is to walk down the street with the intention of staying as awake as possible to whomever we meet. This is training in being emotionally honest with ourselves and becoming more available to others. As we pass people we simply notice whether we open up or shut down. We notice if we feel attraction, aversion, or indifference, without adding anything extra like self-judgment. We might feel compassion toward someone who looks depressed, or cheered up by someone who's smiling to himself. We might feel fear and aversion for another person without even knowing why. Noticing where we open up and where we shut down—without praise or blame—is the basis of our practice. Practicing this way for even one block of a city street can be an eye-opener.

We can take the practice even further by using what comes up as the basis for empathy and understanding. Our own closed feelings like fear or revulsion thus become an opportunity to remember that others also get caught this way. Our open states like friendliness and delight can connect us very personally with the people that we pass on the streets. Either way, we are stretching our hearts.

91

The Truth Is Inconvenient

The difference between theism and nontheism is not whether one does or doesn't believe in God. It's an issue that applies to everyone, including both Buddhists and non-Buddhists. Theism is a deep-seated conviction that there's some hand to hold: if we just do the right things, someone will appreciate us and take care of us. It means thinking there's always going to be a babysitter available when we need one. We all are inclined to abdicate our responsibilities and delegate our authority to something outside ourselves.

Nontheism is relaxing with the ambiguity and uncertainty of the present moment without reaching for anything to protect ourselves. We sometimes think that Buddhist teachings are something outside of ourselves—something to believe in, something to measure up to. However, dharma isn't a belief; it isn't dogma. It is total appreciation of impermanence and change. The teachings disintegrate when we try to grasp them.

We have to experience them without hope. Many brave and compassionate people have experienced them and taught them. The message is fearless; dharma was never meant to be a belief that we blindly follow. Dharma gives us nothing to hold on to at all.

Nontheism is finally realizing that there's no babysitter that you can count on. Just when you get a good one then he or she is gone. Nontheism is realizing that it isn't just babysitters that come and go. The whole of life is like that. This is the truth, and the truth is inconvenient.

92

Abiding in the Fearless State

At a spot called Vulture Peak Mountain, the Buddha presented some revolutionary teachings on the wide-open, groundless dimension of our being, traditionally known as emptiness, absolute bodhichitta, or prajna-paramita.

Many of the students there already had a profound realization of impermanence and egolessness, the truth that nothing—including ourselves—is solid or predictable. They understood the suffering that results from grasping and fixation. They had learned this from Buddha himself; they had experienced its profundity in meditation. But the Buddha knew that our tendency to seek solid ground is deeply rooted. Ego can use anything to maintain the illusion of security, including the belief in insubstantiality and change.

So the Buddha did something shocking. With the teachings on emptiness he pulled the rug out completely, taking his students further into groundlessness. He told them that whatever they believed had to be let go, that dwelling upon any description of reality was a trap. The Buddha's principal message that day was that holding on to *anything* blocks wisdom. *Any* conclusions we might draw must be let go. The only way to fully understand the teachings, the only way to practice them fully, is to abide in unconditional openness, patiently cutting through all our tendencies to hang on.

This instruction—known as the *Heart Sutra*—is a teaching on fearlessness. To the extent that we stop struggling against uncertainty and ambiguity, to that extent we dissolve our fear. Total fearlessness is full enlightenment—wholehearted, open-minded interaction with our world. Meanwhile we train in patiently moving in that direction. By learning to relax with groundlessness, we gradually connect with the mind that knows no fear.

93

The Essential Paradox

In the *Heart Sutra*, one of the Buddha's principal disciples, a monk named Shariputra, begins to question Avalokiteshvara, the bodhisattva of compassion, asking, "In all the words and actions and thoughts of my life, how do I apply the prajnaparamita? What is the key to training in this practice? What view do I take?"

Avalokiteshvara answers with the most famous of Buddhist paradoxes: "Form is emptiness, emptiness also is form. Emptiness is no other than form, form is no other than emptiness." His explanation, like the prajnaparamita itself, is inexpressible, indescribable, inconceivable. Form is that which simply *is* before we project our beliefs onto it. The prajnaparamita represents a completely fresh take, an unfettered mind where anything is possible.

"Form is emptiness" refers to our simple, direct relationship with the immediacy of experience. First we wipe away our preconceptions and then we even have to let go of our belief that we should look at things without preconceptions. In continuing to pull out our own rug, we understand the perfection of things just as they are.

But "emptiness also is form" turns the tables. Emptiness continually manifests as war and peace, as grief, birth, old age, sickness, and death, as well as joy. We are challenged to stay in touch with the heartthrobbing quality of being alive. That's why we train in the relative bodhichitta practices of the four limitless qualities and tonglen. They help us to engage fully in the vividness of life with an open, unclouded mind. Things are as bad and as good as they seem. There's no need to add anything extra.

94

Nothing to Hold On To

Instructions on mindfulness all point to the same thing: being right on the spot nails us. It nails us right to the point of time and space that we are in. When we stop there and don't act out, don't repress, don't blame anyone else, and also don't blame ourselves, then we meet with an open-ended question with no conceptual answer. We also encounter ourselves.

The trick is to keep exploring and not bail out, even when we find that something is not as we thought. That's what we're going to discover again and again and again. Nothing is what we thought. I can say that with great confidence. Emptiness is not what we thought. Neither is mindfulness or fear. Compassion—not what we thought. Love, buddha nature, courage—these are code words for things we don't know in our minds, but any of us could experience them. These are words that point to what life really is when we let things fall apart and let ourselves be nailed to the present moment.

The path of the warrior-bodhisattva is not about going to heaven or a place that's really comfortable. Wanting to find a place where everything's okay is just what keeps us miserable. Always looking for a way to have pleasure and avoid pain is how we keep ourselves in samsara. As long as we believe that there is something that will permanently satisfy our hunger for security, suffering is inevitable. The truth is that things are always in transition. "Nothing to hold on to" is the root of happiness. If we allow ourselves to rest here, we find that it is a tender, nonaggressive, open-ended state of affairs. This is where the path of fearlessness lies.

95

Slogan: "Drive all blames into one"

"Drive all blames into one" is saying, instead of always blaming the other, *own* the feeling of blame, *own* the anger, *own* the loneliness, and make friends with it. Use tonglen practice to see how you can place the anger or the fear or the loneliness in a cradle of loving-kindness; use tonglen to learn how to be gentle to all that stuff. In order to be gentle and create an atmosphere of compassion for yourself, it's necessary to stop talking to yourself about how wrong everything is—or how right everything is, for that matter.

I challenge you to experiment this way: drop the object of your emotion, do tonglen, and see if in fact the intensity of the so-called poison lessens. I have experimented with this, and because my doubt was so strong, for a while it seemed to me that it didn't work. But as my trust grew, I found that that's what happens—the intensity of the emotion lessens, and so does the duration. This happens because the ego begins to be ventilated. We are all primarily addicted to ME. This big solid ME begins to be aerated when we go against the grain and abide with our feelings instead of blaming the other.

The "one" in "Drive all blames into one" is our tendency to protect ourselves: ego-clinging. When we drive all blames into this tendency by staying with our feelings and feeling them fully, the ongoing monolithic ME begins to lighten up, because it is fabricated with our opinions, our moods, and a lot of ephemeral—but at the same time vivid and convincing—stuff.

96

This Very Moment
Is the Perfect Teacher

As we become more open, we might think that it's going to take bigger catastrophes to make us want to exit in our habitual ways. The interesting thing is that, as we open more and more, it's the big ones that immediately wake us up and the little things that catch us off guard. However, no matter the size, color, or shape of the catastrophe, the point is to continue to lean into the discomfort of life and see it clearly rather than try to protect ourselves from it.

In practicing meditation, we're not trying to live up to some kind of ideal—quite the opposite. We're just being with our experience, whatever it is. If our experience is that sometimes we have some kind of perspective, and sometimes we have none, then that's our experience. If sometimes we can approach what scares us, and sometimes we absolutely can't, then that's our experience. "This very moment is the perfect teacher" is really a most profound instruction. Just seeing what's going on—that's the teaching right there. We can be with what's happening and not dissociate. Awakeness is found in our pleasure and our pain, our confusion and our wisdom. It's available in each moment of our weird, unfathomable, ordinary everyday lives.

97

Inviting Your Unfinished Business

You can bring all of your unfinished karmic business right into tonglen practice. In fact, you should invite it in. Suppose that you are involved in a horrific relationship: every time you think of a particular person you feel furious. That is very useful for tonglen! Or perhaps you feel depressed. It was all you could do to get out of bed today. You're so depressed that you want to stay in bed for the rest of your life; you have considered hiding *under* your bed. That is very useful for tonglen practice. The specific fixation should be real, just like that.

You may be formally doing tonglen or just having your coffee, and here comes the object of your fury. You breathe that in. The idea is to develop sympathy for your own confusion. The technique is that you do not blame the object; you also don't blame yourself. Instead, there is just liberated fury—hot, dark, and heavy. Experience it as fully as you can.

Breathe the anger in; remove the object; stop thinking

about him. In fact, he was just a useful catalyst. Now you own the anger completely. You drive all blames into yourself. It takes a lot of bravery, and it's extremely insulting to ego. In fact, it destroys the whole mechanism of ego. So you breathe in.

Then, you breathe out sympathy, relaxation, and spaciousness. Instead of just a small, dark situation, you allow a lot of space for these feelings. Breathing out is like opening up your arms and just letting go. It's fresh air. Then you breathe the rage in again—the dark, heavy hotness of it. Then you breathe out, ventilating the whole thing, allowing a lot of space.

98

Four Methods for Holding Your Seat

When our intention is sincere but the going gets rough, most of us could use some help. We could use some fundamental instruction on how to lighten up and turn around our well-established habits of striking out and blaming.

The four methods for holding our seat provide just such support for developing the patience to stay open to what's happening instead of acting on automatic pilot. These four methods are:

1. *Not setting up the target for the arrow.* The choice is yours: you can strengthen old habits by reacting to irritation with anger, or weaken them by holding your seat.

2. *Connecting with the heart.* Sit with the intensity of the anger and let its energy humble you and make you more compassionate.

3. *Seeing obstacles as teachers*. Right at the point when you're about to blow your top, remember that you're being challenged to stay with edginess and discomfort and to relax where you are.

4. *Regarding all that occurs as a dream*. Contemplate that these outer circumstances, as well as these emotions, as well as this huge sense of ME, are passing and essenceless like a memory, like a movie, like a dream. That realization cuts through panic and fear.

When we find ourselves captured by aggression, we can remember this: we don't have to strike out, nor do we have to repress what we're feeling. We don't have to feel hatred or shame. We can at least begin to question our assumptions. Could it be that whether we are awake or asleep, we are simply moving from one dreamlike state to another?

99

Cultivating Forgiveness

Forgiveness is an essential ingredient of bodhichitta practice. It allows us to let go of the past and make a fresh start. Forgiveness cannot be forced. When we are brave enough to open our hearts to ourselves, however, forgiveness will emerge.

There is a simple practice we can do to cultivate forgiveness. First we acknowledge what we feel—shame, revenge, embarrassment, remorse. Then we forgive ourselves for being human. Then, in the spirit of not wallowing in the pain, we let go and make a fresh start. We don't have to carry the burden with us anymore. We can acknowledge, forgive, and start anew. If we practice this way, little by little we'll learn to abide with the feeling of regret for having hurt ourselves and others. We will also learn self-forgiveness. Eventually, at our own speed, we'll even find our capacity to forgive those who have done us harm. We will discover forgiveness as a natural expression of the open heart, an expression of our basic goodness. This potential is inherent in every moment. Each moment is an opportunity to make a fresh start.

100

Containing the Paradox

Life is glorious, but life is also wretched. Appreciating the gloriousness inspires us, encourages us, cheers us up, gives us a bigger perspective, and energizes us. We feel connected. But if that's all that's happening, we get arrogant and start to look down on others. We make ourselves a big deal and want life to be like that forever. The gloriousness becomes tinged by craving and addiction.

On the other hand, wretchedness—life's painful aspect—softens us up considerably. Knowing pain is an important ingredient of being there for another person. When you are feeling grief, you can look right into somebody's eyes because you feel you haven't got anything to lose—you're just there. The wretchedness humbles us and softens us, but if we were only wretched, we would all be so depressed and hopeless that we wouldn't have enough energy to eat an apple. Gloriousness and wretchedness need each other. One inspires us, the other softens us. They go together.

Atisha said, "Whichever of the two occurs, be patient." Whether it is glorious or wretched, delightful or hateful, be patient. Patience means allowing things to unfold at their own speed rather than jumping in with your habitual response to either pain or pleasure. The real happiness that underlies both gloriousness and wretchedness often gets short-circuited by our jumping too fast into the same habitual pattern.

Patience is not learned in safety. It is not learned when everything is harmonious and going well. When everything is smooth sailing, who needs patience? If you stay in your room with the door locked and the curtains drawn, everything may seem harmonious, but the minute anything doesn't go your way, you blow up. There is no cultivation of patience when your pattern is to just try to seek harmony and smooth everything out. Patience implies willingness to be alive rather than seek harmony.

101

The Sangha

Taking refuge in the sangha—other people on the path of the bodhisattva-warrior—doesn't mean that we join a club where we're all good friends, talk about basic goodness together, nod sagely, and criticize the people who don't believe the way we do. Taking refuge in the sangha means taking refuge in the brotherhood and sisterhood of people who are committed to taking off their armor.

If we live in a family where all the members are committed to taking off their armor, then one of the most powerful vehicles for learning how to do it is the feedback that we give one another, the kindness that we show to one another. Normally when somebody is feeling sorry for herself and beginning to wallow in it, people pat her on the back and say, "Oh, you poor thing," or, "For Pete's sake, get over it." But if you yourself are committed to taking off your armor and you know that the other person is too, there is a way that you can actually give her the gift of dharma. With great kindness and love, out of your own experience of what's possible, you give her the wisdom that somebody else probably gave you the day before when *you* were miserable. You encourage her not to buy into her self-pity but to realize that it's an opportunity to grow, and that everybody goes through this experience.

In other words, the sangha are people committed to helping one another to take off their armor by not encouraging one another's weaknesses or tendencies to keep their armor on. When we see each other collapsing or stubbornly saying, "No, I like this armor," there's an opportunity to say something about the fact that underneath all that armor are a lot of festering sores, and a little bit of sunlight wouldn't hurt a bit. That's the notion of taking refuge in the sangha.

102

Just Like Me
(On-the-Spot Compassion)

As a result of compassion practice we start to have a deeper understanding of the roots of suffering. We aspire not only that the outer manifestations of suffering decrease but also that all of us could stop acting and thinking in ways that escalate ignorance and confusion. We aspire to be free of fixation and closed-mindedness. We aspire to dissolve the myth that we are separate.

It's particularly helpful to take these compassionate aspirations into the marketplace. You can do these practices right in the midst of this paradoxical, unpredictable world. In this way, you can work with your intention and also begin to act. In traditional terms, this is cultivating both levels of bodhichitta: the aspiration and the action. Sometimes this is the only way to make this practice feel relevant to the suffering we continually witness.

I do this sort of thing in all kinds of situations—at the breakfast table, in the meditation hall, at the dentist's office. Standing in the checkout line at the market, I might notice the defiant teenager in front of me and make the aspiration, "May he be free of suffering and its causes." In the elevator with a stranger, I might notice her shoes, her hands, the expression on her face. I contemplate that just like me she doesn't want stress in her life. Just like me she has worries. Through our hopes and fears, our pleasures and pains, we are deeply interconnected.

103

Slogan: "Practice the five strengths, the condensed heart instructions"

There are five strengths we can utilize in our practice of awakening bodhichitta. These are five ways that a warrior increases confidence and inspiration:

1. Cultivating *strong determination* and commitment to relate openly with whatever life presents, including our emotional distress. As warriors-in-training we develop wholehearted determination to use discomfort as an opportunity for awakening, rather than trying to make it disappear. This determination generates strength.

2. Building *familiarization* with the bodhichitta practices by utilizing them in formal practice and on the spot. Whatever happens, our commitment is to use it to awaken our heart.

3. Watering the *seed of bodhichitta* in both delightful and

miserable situations so that our confidence in this positive seed can grow. Sometimes it helps to find little ways that the seed of goodness manifests in our life.

4. Using *reproach*—with kindness and humor—as a way of catching ourselves before we cause harm to self or other. The gentlest method of reproach is asking ourselves, "Have I ever done this before?"

5. Nurturing the habit of *aspiring* for all of us that suffering and its seeds diminish and that wisdom and compassion increase; nurturing the habit of always cultivating our kind heart and open mind. Even when we can't act, we can aspire to find the warrior's strength and ability to love.

104

Reversing the Wheel of Samsara

Every act counts. Every thought and emotion counts too. This moment is all the path we have. This moment is where we apply the teachings. Life is short. Even if we live to be 108, life will still be too short for witnessing all its wonders. The dharma is each act, each thought, each word we speak. Are we at least willing to catch ourselves spinning off and to do that without embarrassment? Do we at least aspire to not consider ourselves a problem, but simply a pretty typical human being who could at that moment give him- or herself a break and stop being so predictable?

The dharma can heal our wounds, our very ancient wounds that come not from original sin but from a misunderstanding so old that we can no longer see it. The instruction is to relate compassionately with where we find ourselves and to begin to see our predicament as workable. We are stuck in patterns of grasping and fixating, which cause the same thoughts and reactions to occur again and again. This is how we project our world. When we see that, even if it's only for one second every three weeks, then we naturally discover the knack of reversing this process of making things solid, the knack of stopping the claustrophobic world as we know it, of putting down our centuries of baggage and stepping into new territory.

How in the world can we do this? The answer is simple. Make the dharma personal, explore it wholeheartedly, and relax.

105

The Path Is the Goal

What does it take to use the life we already have in order to make us wiser rather than more stuck? What is the source of wisdom at a personal, individual level?

The answer to these questions seems to have to do with bringing everything that we encounter to the path. Everything naturally has a ground, path, and fruition. This is like saying that everything has a beginning, middle, and end. But it is also said that the path itself is both the ground and the fruition. The path is the goal.

This path has one very distinct characteristic: it is not prefabricated. It doesn't already exist. The path that we're talking about is the moment-by-moment evolution of our experience, the moment-by-moment evolution of the world of phenomena, the moment-by-moment evolution of our thoughts and emotions. The path is uncharted. It comes into existence moment by moment and at the same time drops away behind us.

When we realize that the path is the goal, there's a sense of workability. Everything that occurs in our confused mind we can regard as the path. Everything is workable.

106

Heightened Neurosis

We might assume that as we train in bodhichitta our habitual patterns will start to unwind—that day by day, month by month, we'll be more open-minded, more flexible, more of a warrior. But what actually happens with ongoing practice is that our patterns intensify. This is called "heightened neurosis." It just happens. We catch the scent of groundlessness, and despite our wishes to remain steady, open, and flexible, we hold on tight in very habitual ways.

For example, we may develop a new self-critical story line based on spiritual ideals. The warrior training becomes just one more way to feel that we never measure up. Or we use our training to increase our sense of being special, to build up our self-image and increase our arrogance and pride. Or perhaps we sincerely wish to surrender our useless baggage, but in the process, we use the teachings themselves to distance ourselves from the chaotic, unsettling quality of our lives. We try to use our spiritual training to avoid the queasy feeling in our gut.

The point is that we will bring our habitual ways of gluing ourselves together right into bodhichitta practice, right into the training in *un*gluing. But because of our practice, we can start to look compassionately at what we do. What is happening to us psychologically? Do we feel inadequate? Do we continue to believe in our same old dramas? Are we using spirituality to bypass what scares us? It's easy not to see where we are still seeking ground in the same old ways. We have to gradually develop the confidence that it is liberating to let go. Continually we train in maitri. It takes time to develop enthusiasm for how remaining open really feels.

107

Compassionate Inquiry

When our attitude toward fear becomes more welcoming and inquisitive, a fundamental shift occurs. Instead of spending our lives tensing up, we learn that we can connect with the freshness of the moment and relax.

The practice is compassionate inquiry into our moods, our emotions, our thoughts. Compassionate inquiry into our reactions and strategies is fundamental to the process of awakening. We are encouraged to be curious about the neurosis that's bound to kick in when our coping mechanisms start falling apart. This is how we get to the place where we stop believing in our personal myths, the place where we are not always divided against ourselves, always resisting our own energy. This is how we learn to abide in basic goodness.

It's an ongoing practice. From the instant we begin training as a bodhisattva until we completely trust the freedom of our unconditional, unbiased mind, we are surrendering moment by moment to whatever is happening in this very instant of time. With precision and gentleness, we surrender our cherished ways of regarding ourselves and others, our cherished ways of holding it all together, our cherished ways of blocking our tender heart. In the process of doing this again and again over many challenging and inspiring years, we develop an appetite for groundlessness.

108

Slogan: "Always maintain only a joyful mind"

"Always maintain only a joyful mind" might sound like an impossible aspiration. As one man said to me, "Always is a very long time." Yet as we train in unblocking our hearts, we'll find that every moment contains the free-flowing openness and warmth that characterize unlimited joy.

This is the path we take in cultivating joy: learning not to armor our basic goodness, learning to appreciate what we have. Most of the time we don't do this. Rather than appreciate where we are, we continually struggle and nurture our dissatisfaction. It's like trying to get the flowers to grow by pouring cement on the garden.

But as we use the bodhichitta practices to train, we may come to the point where we see the magic of the present moment; we may gradually wake up to the truth that we have always been warriors living in a sacred world. This is the ongoing experience of limitless joy. We won't always experience this, it's true. But year by year it becomes more and more accessible.

DEDICATION OF MERIT

By this merit, may all attain omniscience,
May it defeat the enemy, wrongdoing,
From the stormy waves of birth, old age, sickness, and death,
From the ocean of samsara, may I free all beings.

By the confidence of the golden sun of the great east,
May the lotus garden of the Rigden's wisdom bloom.
May the dark ignorance of sentient beings be dispelled.
May all beings enjoy profound brilliant glory.

GLOSSARY

ASPIRATION PRACTICE A practice in which we aspire to expand the four limitless qualities of loving-kindness, compassion, joy, and equanimity by extending them to others.

BODHICHITTA (Skt.) The awakened heart of loving-kindness and compassion. *Absolute bodhichitta* is our natural state, experienced as the basic goodness that links us to every other living being. It has been defined as openness, ultimate truth, our true nature, soft spot, tender heart, or simply what *is*. It combines the qualities of compassion, unconditional openness, and keen intelligence. It is free from concepts, opinions, and dualistic notions of "self" and "other." *Relative bodhichitta* is the courage to realize this tender openhearted quality by tapping into our capacity to love and care for others.

BUDDHA (Skt.) "Awakened one." The founder of Buddhism, a prince named Siddhartha Gautama, born in the sixth century BCE in what is now Nepal. He left his palace at the age of twenty-nine and set out on a spiritual journey that resulted in his attaining enlightenment and becoming the Buddha. He devoted the rest of his life to showing others how to experience this awakening and liberation from suffering. We too are buddhas. We are the awakened ones—the ones who continually leap, who continually open, who continually go forward.

DHARMA (Skt.) "Cosmic law." The teachings of the Buddha, the truth of what is.

THE EIGHT WORDLY DHARMAS These are four pairs of opposites—four things that we like and become attached to and four things that we don't like and try to avoid. The eight worldly dharmas are pleasure and pain, praise and blame, fame and disgrace, gain and loss. The basic message is that when we are caught up in the eight worldly dharmas, we suffer.

THE FOUR LIMITLESS QUALITIES Love, compassion, joy, and equanimity. They are called limitless because our capacity to experience and extend them has no limit.

LOJONG (Tib.) "Mind training," our inheritance from the eleventh-century Buddhist master Atisha Dipankara. Mind training includes two elements: sending-and-taking practice (tonglen), in which we take in pain and send out pleasure, and slogan practice, in which we use pithy slogans to reverse our habitual attitude of self-absorption. These methods instruct us in using what might seem like our greatest obstacles—anger, resentment, fear, jealousy—as fuel for awakening.

MAITRI (Skt.) "Unconditional loving-kindness." A direct, unconditional relationship with all aspects of ourselves and others. Without loving-kindness for ourselves, it is difficult, if not impossible, to genuinely feel it for others.

PARAMITAS (Skt.) "That which has reached the other shore." These are six qualities that take us beyond our habitual ways of seeking solidity and security. The six paramitas are generosity, patience, discipline, exertion, meditation, and prajna, or wisdom.

PRAJNA (Skt.) "Wisdom." As the sixth paramita, prajna is the highest form of knowledge, the wisdom that experiences reality directly, without concept.

SAMSARA (Skt.) "Journeying." The vicious cycle of suffering that results from the mistaken belief in the solidity and permanence of self and other.

THE THREE JEWELS The Buddha, the dharma, and the sangha.

TONGLEN (Tib.) "Sending and receiving." Also described as exchanging self for other. In the practice of tonglen, we breathe in whatever feels bad and send out whatever feels good.

SANGHA (Skt.) "Crowd, host." The Buddhist community. All others on the path of the bodhisattva-warrior.

WARROIR-BODHISATTVA One who aspires to act from the awakened heart of bodhichitta for the benefit of others.

BIBLIOGRAPHY

BOOKS FROM WHICH THESE TEACHINGS WERE EXCERPTED OR ADAPTED

Chödrön, Pema. *The Wisdom of No Escape and the Path of Loving-Kindness*. Boston: Shambhala Publications, 1991; London: Element, 2005.

———. *Start Where You Are: A Guide to Compassionate Living*. Boston: Shambhala Publications, 1994; London: Element, 2005.

———. *When Things Fall Apart: Heart Advice for Difficult Times*. Boston: Shambhala Publications, 1996; London: Element, 2005.

———. *The Places That Scare You: A Guide to Fearlessness in Difficult Times*. Boston: Shambhala Publications, 2001; London: Element, 2005.

GENERAL TEACHINGS ON BODHICHITTA

Patrul Rinpoche. *The Words of My Perfect Teacher*. Translated by the Padmakara Translation Group. Boston: Shambhala Publications, 1998, pp. 195–261.

Shantideva. *The Way of the Bodhisattva*. Translated by the Padmakara Translation Group. Boston: Shambhala Publications, 1997.

———. *A Guide to the Bodhisattva's Way of Life*. Translated by Stephen Batchelor. Dharamsala, India: Library of Tibetan Works and Archives, 1998.

Sogyal Rinpoche. *The Tibetan Book of Living and Dying.* Edited by Patrick Gaffney and Andrew Harvey. San Francisco: HarperSanFrancisco, 1993.

Trungpa, Chögyam. *Cutting Through Spiritual Materialism.* Boston: Shambhala Publications, 1987, pp. 167–216.

———. *The Myth of Freedom.* Boston: Shambhala Publications, 1988, pp. 103–126.

The Four Limitless Qualities

Kamalashila. *Meditation: The Buddhist Way of Tranquility and Insight.* Glasgow: Windhorse, 1992, pp. 23–32, 192–206.

Longchenpa. *Kindly Bent to Ease Us.* Translated by H. V. Guenther. Berkeley, Calif.: Dharma Publications, 1975–76, pp. 106–122.

Patrul Rinpoche. *The Words of My Perfect Teacher.* Translated by the Padmakara Translation Group. Boston: Shambhala Publications, 1998, pp. 195–217.

Salzberg, Sharon. *Lovingkindness: The Revolutionary Art of Happiness.* Boston: Shambhala Publications, 1995.

Thich Nhat Hanh. *Teachings on Love.* Berkeley, Calif.: Parallax Press, 1997.

The Lojong Slogans

Chödrön, Pema. *Start Where You Are: A Guide to Compassionate Living.* Boston: Shambhala Publications, 1994.

Khyentse, Dilgo. *Enlightened Courage.* Ithaca, N.Y.: Snow Lion Publications, 1993.

Kongtrul, Jamgon. *The Great Path of Awakening: A Commentary on the Mahayana Teaching of the Seven Points of Mind Training*. Boston: Shambhala Publications, 1987.

Trungpa, Chögyam. *Training the Mind and Cultivating Loving Kindness*. Edited by Judith L. Lief. Boston: Shambhala Publications, 1993.

Wallace, Alan B. *A Passage from Solitude: Training the Mind in a Life Embracing the World*. Edited by Zara Houshmand. Ithaca, N.Y.: Snow Lion Publications, 1992.

TONGLEN PRACTICE

Chödron, Pema. *Tonglen: The Path of Transformation*. Edited by Tingdzin Ötro. Halifax, Nova Scotia: Vajradhatu Publications, 2000.

Sogyal Rinpoche. *The Tibetan Book of Living and Dying*. Edited by Patrick Gaffney and Andrew Harvey. San Francisco: HarperSanFrancisco, 1993, pp. 201–208.

ADDITIONAL READING

Beck, Joko. *Everyday Zen: Love and Work*. Edited by Steve Smith. San Francisco: HarperSanFrancisco, 1989.

———. *Nothing Special: Living Zen*. San Francisco: HarperSanFrancisco, 1994.

Bayda, Ezra. *Being Zen: Bringing Meditation to Life*. Boston: Shambhala Publications, 2002.

Trungpa, Chögyam. *Shambhala: The Sacred Path of the Warrior*. Boston: Shambhala Publications, 1984.

RESOURCES

FOR INFORMATION ABOUT MEDITATION instruction or to find a practice center near you, please contact one of the following:

Shambhala International
1084 Tower Road
Halifax, NS
Canada B3H 2Y5
phone: (902) 425-4275 ext. 10
fax: (902) 423-2750

website: www.shambhala.org (this website contains information about the more than 100 centers affiliated with Shambhala)

Shambhala Europe
Annostrasse 27
50678 Cologne, Germany
phone: 49-0-700-108-000-00
e-mail: europe@shambhala.org
website: www.shambhala-europe.org

Karmê Chöling
369 Patneaude Lane
Barnet, VT 05821
phone: (802) 633-2384
fax: (802) 633-3012
e-mail: karmecholing@shambhala.org

Shambhala Mountain Center
4921 Country Road 68C
Red Feather Lakes, Co 80545
phone: (970) 881-2184
fax: (970) 881-2909
e-mail: shambhalamountain@shambhala.org

Gampo Abbey
Pleasant Bay, NS
Canada B0E 2P0
phone: (902) 224-2752
e-mail: office@gampoabbey.org

Naropa University is the only accredited, Buddhist-inspired university in North America. For more information, contact:

Naropa University
2130 Arapahoe Avenue
Boulder, CO 80302
phone: (303) 444-0202
website: www.naropa.edu

Audio-and videotape recordings of talks and seminars by Pema Chödrön are available from:

Great Path Tapes and Books
330 East Van Hoesen Boulevard
Portage, MI 49002
phone: (269) 384-4167
fax: (425) 940-8456
e-mail: gptapes@aol.com
website: www.pemachodrontapes.org

Kalapa Recordings
1084 Tower Road
Halifax, NS
Canada B3H 2Y5
phone: (269) 384-4167
fax: (425) 940-8456
e-mail: shop@shambhala.org
website: www.shambhalashop.com

Sounds True
735 Walnut Street
Boulder, CO 80302
phone: (800) 333-9185
website: www.soundstrue.com

Cards printed with each of the mind-training slogans, as well as a poster for use in one's practice, are available from:

Samadhi Store
Karmê Chöling
R.R. 1, Box 3
Barnet, VT 05821
phone: (800) 331-7751
e-mail: order@samadhicushions.com

Ziji Catalog
9148 Kerry Road
Boulder, CO 80303
phone: (800) 565-8470
e-mail: ziji@csd.net

Drala Books and Gifts
1567 Grafton Street
Halifax, NS
Canada B3J 2C3
phone: (902) 422-2504

The *Shambhala Sun* is a bimonthly Buddhist magazine founded by Chögyam Trungpa Rinpoche. For a subscription or sample copy, contact:

Shambhala Sun
P.O. Box 3377
Champlain, NY 12919-9871
phone (toll free): (877) 786-1950
website: www.shambhalasun.com

Buddhamdharma: *The Practicioner's Quarterly* is an in-depth, practice-oriented jouirnal offering teachings from all Buddhist traditions. For a subscripton or sample copy, contact:

Buddhadharma
P.O. Box 3377
Champlain, NY 12919-9871
phone (toll free): (877) 786-1950
website: www.buddhadharma.com